Phil Dampier has been writing about the royal family for 21 years. Between 1986 and 1991 he covered the royal beat for *The Sun*. He established a reputation for breaking major exclusive stories, and is renowned for his far-reaching contacts. As a freelance journalist for the last 16 years, he has travelled to more than 40 countries, following members of the House of Windsor, and his articles have been published in dozens of newspapers and magazines worldwide. He is currently royal editor of *New Idea*, one of Australia's biggest selling magazines. He lives in Kent with his partner Ann.

Ashley Walton was the royal correspondent of the *Daily Express* from 1979 to 1992. He travelled to every continent covering numerous tours, including the Queen and Prince Philip in India, Africa and China. He was one of the first reporters to identify a young Lady Diana Spencer as a future royal bride, and covered her last tour with Prince Charles to Korea in 1992. He was also among the first to reveal the romance between Prince Andrew and Sarah Ferguson. He lives in Hertfordshire with his wife Joan and their two sons.

By the same authors:

Duke of Hazard – The Wit and Wisdom of Prince Philip, The Book Guild, 2006

WHAT'S IN THE QUEEN'S HANDBAG

(And Other Royal Secrets)

Phil Dampier and
Ashley Walton

Book Guild Publishing
Sussex, England

First published in Great Britain in 2007 by
The Book Guild Ltd
Pavilion View
19 New Road
Brighton BN1 1UF

Twelfth printing 2012

Typesetting in Garamond by
Keyboard Services, Luton, Bedfordshire

Printed in Great Britain by
CPI Antony Rowe

A catalogue record for this book is available from
The British Library

ISBN 978 1 84624 194 9

Contents

Sources and Acknowledgements

The authors would like to thank Bob Cameron, a legendary figure in Australian journalism, for suggesting the title of this book. We would also like to thank our long-standing contacts who, over the years, have been the source of many stories – they know who they are! We are also grateful to material from the following books:

Burgess, Major Colin, *Behind Palace Doors*. John Blake Publishing, London, 2006

Crawford, Marion, *The Little Princesses*. Orion, London, 2002

Hoey, Brian, *Her Majesty Fifty Regal Years*. HarperCollins, London, 2001

Hoey, Brian, *At Home With the Queen*. HarperCollins, London, 2002

Handbag: Order of the Handbag

'The Queen has a collection of around 200 bags...'

What's in the Queen's handbag? It's a question that's intrigued royal watchers for decades. And now this fascinating book gives the answer, as well as dozens of other secrets of the House of Windsor.

Thousands of books and millions of words have been written about the British monarchy. But our appetite for intimate details of this extraordinary family remains insatiable. And why? The reason is probably because the characters in this real life soap opera are normal people placed in an unnatural setting. We can't all live in Buckingham Palace, but it's reassuring to know that the Queen serves her breakfast cereal from a Tupperware container, just like the rest of us.

Co-author Phil Dampier has been writing about the royal family for more than 20 years, first for *The Sun*, and then as a freelance journalist. He says: 'For the last fifteen years I have written articles for many newspapers and magazines around the world, but without doubt the biggest selling feature has been the contents of Her Majesty's handbag! It seems incredible but people are more curious about trivia than major matters of state or the role of monarchy. I suppose women in particular feel they can judge someone's personality and tastes by the contents of their handbag. Every couple of years a magazine somewhere in the world will want to run the article, so it's about time it was put in a book. I was lucky to find a close aide of the Queen who was well placed to know the truth about what the

Queen kept in her bags, and I say bags, because she has around two hundred of them! But the immense interest convinced me that people just can't get enough of the royals' private lives and, for good or bad, will be just as anxious to get a "fix" of gossip in the 21st century as they were in the last one.'

Queen Elizabeth II was dubbed a 'fashion icon' on a state visit to Rome in 2000 and the style-conscious Italians were as curious as the rest of us about her handbags. She wowed her hosts at a state dinner (after being served goat!) and another function with two beautiful bags in brown and dark navy kid. Designer Miuccia Prada, whose clients include Victoria Beckham, hailed the Queen as 'one of the most elegant women in the world'. And Carla Fendi, whose handbags sell all over the world, declared: 'She has such a personal style – I would love to make a special bag for her.' One newspaper put a team of reporters on the case for a week – but could only find out that she keeps lipstick in her bag.

So here, for the benefit of those frustrated Italians, and everyone else, is the full truth:

The Queen has a collection of around 200 bags, some of them 30 or 40 years old. She does not normally carry money, a cheque book, credit cards, car keys or a passport (because she doesn't have one!). But the first item she tends to pull out of the bag at meal times is an S-shaped meat hook. Not to hang up a pheasant shot by Prince Philip that morning but to secure the bag itself. The hook is placed on the table's edge and watch out any clumsy servant who knocks it off!

The Queen has always been superstitious and carries an amazing array of good luck charms, mostly given to her by her four children, Charles, Anne, Andrew and Edward. They are often on an animal theme including horses, miniature dogs, tiny saddles and brass whips.

Like any proud mother she keeps a selection of family photos – a particular favourite is one of Prince Andrew when he safely returned from the 1982 Falklands war after serving as a helicopter pilot in the Royal Navy. The Queen worried herself sick during the South Atlantic conflict and is forever grateful that her favourite son came back unharmed.

Other staples include a tube of mints (always on hand to soothe a tickly throat before yet another speech), a packet of doggie choc-drops for her beloved pets (how could she forget the corgis?), and, to avoid wasting time, a couple of crosswords snipped out of the daily papers by servants.

The Queen uses a fountain pen and frowns upon biros, banning the staff from using them in her presence.

One of her most personal and prized possessions is a small metal make-up case which Prince Philip made for her as a wedding gift. She has treasured it for 60 years, opening it for a quick dab of powder or a touch of lipstick before – or sometimes during – public appearances. The Queen's tendency to powder her nose at the dinner table apparently shocked the sensibilities of Canada's former Governor General Adrienne Clarkson. In her memoirs, *Heart Matters*, Miss Clarkson, who was Her Majesty's representative in Canada from October 1999 to September 2005, wrote: 'I was interested to see the Queen powder her nose at the table. In Canada we had always been brought up to believe that we were never supposed to do anything to our make-up at the table, so I am simply passing on the information for those who like to keep up-to-date with royal etiquette.' Thank you, Miss Clarkson!

Not wanting to miss a photo-opportunity, the Queen sometimes slips in a small camera and has frequently astounded world leaders by suddenly snapping them for her personal album.

Add in a mirror, diary and address book, sunglasses,

reading glasses, and, like any good girl scout, a penknife, and it is obvious why no ordinary size bag will do. For some walkabouts and other events a smaller bag will, of course, suffice.

Never forget the Queen's wonderful sense of humour. At Royal Ascot in July 2004 she deliberately opened up her bag of the day in full view of photographers and revealed ... nothing inside but a purse! Said one courtier: 'She has a superb sense of fun and knows she is renowned for not carrying cash, so this was her little joke.' A joke she repeated in April 2006 when she produced a ten pound note from her handbag for the collection at a service in St George's Chapel, Windsor, to celebrate her 80th birthday.

London-based firm Launer has had the royal warrant to supply the Queen's bags for the past 40 years, and chairman Gerald Bodmer, who bought the company in 1981, credits her patronage for its success. Hand-made at a factory in Walsall, the bags, made from soft calf, lizard, ostrich or alligator skin, cost around £500 each and come in many different colours. Each is distinguished by Launer's intertwined gold rope logo, which is often worked into the clasps. The Queen favours high quality leathers, mainly dark in colour, but is no Imelda Marcos and does not buy a new handbag with every new pair of shoes. In fact, she still uses most of the bags she owns. Other notable customers include Baroness Thatcher, Dame Judi Dench, the Crown Princess of Japan and Sophie, Countess of Wessex. Princess Diana and Princess Margaret were also fans. In March 1991 the Queen visited the Walsall factory and spent an entire afternoon meeting skilled craftsmen and seeing the manufacturing process.

As any woman will tell you, there is much more to a handbag than its style or practicality. Indeed, a leading British psychiatrist has suggested that Her Majesty clings to her bags out of a basic insecurity. Dr Dennis Friedman, author of *Inheritance, A Psychological History of the Royal Family*, said: 'She takes her bag everywhere. Despite being one of the wealthiest and most loved women in the world she is extremely insecure. Although she had a happy childhood, the burden of becoming Queen when she was just twenty-five and mourning her father left her with a deep sense of insecurity. This feeling still haunts her despite decades on the throne. So she clings to her handbag for security, like a child hangs on to a favourite teddy bear or blanket. A handbag is a symbolic womb – it carries everything a woman holds dear. The only place where she tends not to carry it is at Balmoral, her castle in Scotland. There she is surrounded by happy memories and feels secure.'

It is not just the contents of the bag or its comfort

value that matter to the monarch – she also uses it to send out coded messages to her staff and guests. At lunches and dinners guests are told beforehand that when the Queen places her bag on the table, the event is nearing its end, with probably another five minutes to go. On walkabouts she drops the bag to one side in a certain manner, indicating to staff that she is about to move on. A lady-in-waiting then moves in to keep talking to the person concerned so that they are not offended.

If the Queen puts her bag on the floor during a banquet she is telling her aides that the person next to her is boring, and again, a lady-in-waiting will come to the rescue. The sight courtiers most like to see is the bag dangling from her left crooked arm, with her gloves held in the other hand. That indicates everything is going well and she is happy and relaxed.

Things were obviously going well on that tour of Italy as *La Republica* carried a front page article entitled 'Ode to the Queen's handbag' and noted: 'There it is. That disturbing object, firmly attached to her left forearm. The secret of her regality is in that little royal, but so ordinary, accessory.'

In June 2006, during celebrations for her 80th birthday, the Queen herself acknowledged the importance of her handbag. Buckingham Palace was thrown open to 2,000 youngsters for a party to celebrate favourite children's literary characters, and more than 50 showbiz stars appeared in a specially written play *The Queen's Handbag*. The theme was simple – the bag had been stolen and goodies then fought baddies to retrieve it. Eventually the bag was recovered so that she could pull out her reading glasses and make a speech at the end. 'I am delighted to have my handbag back,' she said. 'I do like happy endings.'

Ghosts: *The Crown Ghouls!*

'She came down the stairs at Sandringham with a sheet over her head...'

The Queen is deeply religious and believes that the vows she made at her 1953 coronation were witnessed by God and cannot be broken. It is for that reason that she will never abdicate, and poor old Prince Charles will have to wait until she dies before he becomes king. If the Queen dies at the same age as her mother – 101 – Charles will be nearly 80 before he comes to the throne, unless of course he dies first! But nothing will change Elizabeth's mind. She is acutely aware of her place in history, and will want to live long enough to pass Queen Victoria's record of 63 years as monarch.

This spirituality and fascination with the past probably accounts for the Queen's superstitious nature and belief in ghosts. A courtier revealed: 'The Queen firmly believes in ghosts and often tells how they are present in all of her homes. She is not frightened of them, just simply fascinated.'

Her Majesty is convinced that the ghost of Elizabeth I haunts her favourite home, Windsor Castle. She and her younger sister Princess Margaret first saw the ghost in the Green Corridor linking ancient apartments when they were children. Born in 1533, the daughter of Henry VIII and Anne Boleyn died aged 69 in 1603 after a reign of 44 years. She was terrified of catching the plague, and a gallows was built at Windsor where anyone suspected of having the disease was hanged without argument. Several victims are still said to haunt the thousand-room castle. Added the courtier: 'The Queen has a great sense of history and her own part in it. I expect the idea that she will spend eternity as a ghost in her favourite home when she passes on would appeal to her greatly!'

The first performance of Shakespeare's play *The Merry Wives of Windsor* was staged for Elizabeth I in the castle. Herne the Hunter, featured in the play, is a legendary ghost at Windsor. One story says he was a man caught hunting in Henry VIII's woods and was dealt with accordingly. But a more interesting tale claims he was a keeper in Windsor Forest who, wounded by a stag, became insane, ran for miles unclothed and hanged himself from a tree near the castle. The original oak was felled during the reign of George III, who on discovering this decreed that a nearby tree should be called Herne's Oak. This was blown down in 1863 but Queen Victoria planted another one. Eventually Edward VII investigated the tales and planted another tree on the original site – it stands today by the sixth hole of the castle golf course. On fluffing a shot there Prince Andrew once remarked: 'I feel like hanging myself too!'

Royal servants are a hardy breed, but even in modern times several have been terrified by unexpected spectres.

In 1996 footman Shaun Croasdale ran screaming through the corridors of Sandringham Palace, the Queen's home in Norfolk, after seeing the ghost of Her Majesty's favourite servant who had died a year earlier. Shaun, then 40, dropped several bottles of expensive vintage wine and fled in horror after seeing the spirit of Tony Jarred. Within minutes the Queen had heard about his ordeal, and invited him to tell her all about his experience. She listened

for several minutes as Shaun explained how he had turned round and seen Tony 'as plain as daylight' dressed in his familiar blue apron he wore in the cellars. Shaun was so scared that another member of staff had to go back to the cellar to fetch that day's drinks following the incident shortly after Christmas. According to servants, the Queen told him not to worry and was fascinated by his story. Tony had died aged 60 after 38 years of loyal service.

An insider commented: 'The Queen was very fond of Tony and took comfort from the fact that he was still around. She believed every word of Shaun's story – there was never any question of him being sacked for going potty. Several spirits have been seen at Sandringham, which is one of the most haunted royal homes. For years servants to the Queen have seen strange goings on in their rooms. Clothes and ornaments have moved around in front of their eyes without explanation. And whenever something odd happens the Queen is the first who wants to know all about it.

'She is not the only royal to see ghosts. About twenty years ago Prince Charles went into the library at Sandringham with his then valet Ken Stronach. They both felt very cold and were convinced someone was behind them. But when they looked round no-one was there. They just looked amazed at each other, said "oh heck" and ran out as fast as they could! Charles still talks about it today – he was petrified.'

Angela Kelly, former housemaid and currently the Queen's dresser, was terrified of ghosts, but made the mistake of letting her colleagues know. For years they scared her with spooky stories but one day she decided to take revenge. 'She came down the stairs at Sandringham with a sheet over her head and crept up behind some maids,' said one footman. 'It was quite dark and late at night and they just jumped out of their skins! Angela thought it was hilarious after all they had put her through. So many of us have had experiences that we all believe in ghosts. Sandringham has more than two hundred and seventy rooms but Windsor is the worst – parts are nearly a thousand years old and very scary. The Queen has never had them exorcised because she feels they are harmless and add character to the place.'

For centuries King Henry VIII's fifth wife Catherine Howard is said to have haunted his home Hampton Court Palace in West London. She was beheaded at the Tower of London for adultery with courtier Thomas Culpepper, but while awaiting her fate at Hampton Court she escaped and ran along a 15-metre gallery to hammer on Henry's door, begging for mercy. Some claim to have heard her screams, and others to have seen her running, her white face contorted in agony. Her appeal fell on deaf ears and she was dragged away by guards to be executed on 13 February 1542.

In recent years at least two women tourists have fainted in the 'haunted gallery' complaining of suddenly feeling cold. Others have heard noises or seen an apparition fleeing along the gallery. So in 2000 psychologist Dr Richard Wiseman, a professional investigator of the paranormal, conducted experiments to see if he could find any ghosts at Hampton Court. Using thermal cameras, electromagnetic and light sensors, Dr Wiseman, from Hertfordshire University, also interviewed 1,000 visitors for their experiences.

'I was amazed by the number of unusual responses we got,' he said. 'Around fifty per cent of people had an unusual experience and about a fifth felt a ghostly presence.'

Three years later an extraordinary figure in period costume was captured on CCTV at Hampton Court and workers there were baffled. The spectre, in a long, fur-trimmed coat, was seen shutting a fire door, but no human was present at the time. The appearance remains a mystery. But sadly, Dr Wiseman's research concluded that two 'cold spots' at the palace probably accounted for the strange sightings. His thermal imaging cameras revealed that the gallery contained two places where the temperature was a degree or two lower than the rest of the passageway.

'The haunted gallery has a lot of concealed doors and they appear to be causing some unusual patterns of cold air,' he said. 'Some of these ghostly encounters may have been people walking into a column of cold air. If you suddenly feel cold for no apparent reason, and you happen to believe in ghosts, you may believe that you are in a haunted place. That could cause an even more extreme experience such as hearing a scream or seeing a ghost.'

Dr Wiseman may have his theories, but nothing will alter the Queen's belief that she lives with the company of royal ghosts from centuries past.

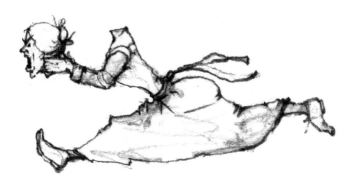

Dogs: The Royal Wruffians

'A good hosing down.'

When the Queen was seen wearing a sticking plaster on her hand late in 2006, there was, inevitably, speculation as to how she had injured herself, and concern for her health as she turned 80. But to seasoned royal watchers the answer should have been obvious – she had been hurt breaking up a fight among her beloved corgis!

It is often said that the Queen prefers the company of dogs and horses to people. This probably stems from her childhood when she and her younger sister Margaret led an isolated existence, and in the absence of many friends, they became much closer to their pets.

As far as the monarch is concerned her corgis can do no wrong. But that's not always how servants and visitors to royal palaces see it. Looking after as many as seven or eight corgis at a time is no easy task and for two footmen it is one of their most important duties.

At Buckingham Palace the dogs sleep in their own room, next to the Page's Pantry just outside the Queen's bedroom. They have wicker baskets, raised slightly off the ground to avoid draughts. Sometimes Her Majesty even allows some of them to sleep in her room.

Normally a footman takes them into the garden first thing in the morning to 'do their business'. But inevitably some will occasionally misbehave inside, and staff then have the unpleasant task of cleaning up the mess. Blotting paper and soda water are on hand to remove stains.

Soda-siphons have also been turned on the pooches themselves by frustrated footmen. 'When we got fed up with them snapping around our heels we would give them a good hosing down,' said one retired servant. 'The Queen did sometimes seem curious as to why the dogs were wet when it hadn't been raining but we never told her the truth – she would have gone mental.'

'Soda siphons have also been turned on the pooches themselves by frustrated footmen.'

The Queen did 'go mental' in 1999 when one of her footmen got the corgis drunk on whisky and gin! Under the typically brilliant headline 'Flunky got the corgis drunky' *The Sun*, Britain's biggest-selling daily tabloid, told how the Queen's footman Matthew King was demoted after it was discovered he was spiking the dogs' food and water as a prank. Another servant said: 'He thought it was funny to see the dogs staggering about. He lost his position and was lucky not to get sacked. The Queen did not see the funny side to put it mildly.'

King, then 28, was downgraded to the rank of a normal footman and lost several privileges.

Suspicions were aroused two years earlier when one corgi – Phoenix – died during the Queen's summer break at Balmoral in Scotland. A routine post-mortem examination carried out by a vet on the 14-year-old revealed traces of alcohol in its blood. King's other duties included responsibility for Her Majesty's drinks trolley – groaning with whisky, gin and other spirits. A colleague claimed: 'Matthew made sure he only played the prank when the Queen was away. He thought it was all a bit of fun, which didn't do the dogs any harm. But he was well and truly in the doghouse when he was finally found out.'

It was hardly surprising that King got fed up with his charges – although his methods of dealing with them were somewhat unconventional. At the time

'He thought it was funny to see the dogs staggering about.'

the Queen had four corgis Pharos, Kelpie, Swift and Emma, as well as four dorgis (corgi-dachshund crosses) Harris, Brandy, Cider and Berry. Britain's top dog 'shrink' Dr Roger Mugford had frequently told the Queen that she had too many dogs together, and they formed a pack mentality. This could make them snappy and attack people, or fight among themselves. But there is only so much advice you can give to your monarch without being sent to the tower!

Certainly King wasn't the first or last servant to fall foul of the pampered pets. The Queen's obsession with corgis began in 1933 when as a seven-year-old she fell in love with one belonging to Viscount Weymouth. When she was 18 her parents gave her Susan, her first corgi, and the 30 or so others that have followed were descended from her. Susan even accompanied Elizabeth and Philip in 1947 on the first part of their honeymoon to Broadlands, the Mountbatten family home in Hampshire. She was bundled into their open carriage at the last moment as they rode through the streets of London and headed for Waterloo Station to catch a train.

It was Susan who began the tradition of nipping servants when she sank her teeth into the leg of clock-winder Leonard Hubbard. She was hauled off by another worker and Leonard needed hospital treatment to a one-inch gash. Susan went on to bite several other people, including Grenadier Guardsman Alfred Edge while he was on sentry

duty outside Buckingham Palace. She also attacked a policeman, whose hefty kick at his aggressor was unfortunately witnessed by the owner. The Queen reportedly told him: 'Don't you ever let me see you do that to a dog again.'

Susan was not above chewing leather upholstery in royal Land Rovers, but when she died aged 14 in 1959 the heartbroken Queen designed her gravestone and had her buried at Sandringham. It read: 'Susan. Died 26th January 1959. For almost 15 years the faithful companion of the Queen.'

Susan's grandson Whisky soon followed in her paw-prints and disgraced himself by tearing the seat out of a soldier's trousers. And so it went on, with cats not getting a look in. (When the Queen was given a pedigree Siamese, it was given to a cook for adoption.)

'Whisky soon followed in her pawprints and disgraced himself by tearing the seat out of a soldier's trousers.'

In 1989 the Queen's favourite dog Chipper was savaged to death by one of the Queen Mother's corgis. Chipper, a 12-year-old dorgi (the result of cross-breeding with Princess Margaret's dachshund Pipkin) was set upon at Windsor Castle by a pack of dogs led by Ranger. One servant reported: 'It was a very nasty fight and poor Chipper was ripped to shreds.'

Animal psychologist Dr Mugford was called in from his clinic in Surrey and immediately diagnosed the problem – too many dogs! He said: 'The Queen has eight and the Queen Mum three so when they get together there are far too many. Chipper had been leader of the pack but as he got old the others saw their chance and pounced. It happens in the wild and is rather like getting the bull elephant out of the way.'

One servant said at the time: 'Ranger has a nasty streak and should be put down but the Queen Mum loves him and he even sleeps on the foot of her bed. It would be too upsetting for her, so everyone has to put up with him.'

At least Chipper no longer had to suffer at the hands of footman Paul Burrell, later to achieve fame as Princess Diana's butler. A retired servant, who used to work with Burrell revealed: 'Chipper had an extraordinary reaction to the sound of zips being undone and done up. To keep us amused Paul would keep on unzipping his flies, which would

'To keep us amused Paul would keep on unzipping his flies...'

send this corgi mad. Sometimes we would all join in, making the poor thing delirious!'

Perhaps Burrell was seeking revenge for an earlier experience he had suffered with the dogs. When he took nine corgis for a walk on a snowy day at Sandringham they each wanted to be first out of the door. 'As I turned to shut the door with one hand, nine leads yanked me the other way,' he recalled in his book *A Royal Duty*. 'I fell, banged my head on the steps and was knocked unconscious as the corgis scurried off into the snow. The next thing I was waking up with the faces of the Queen and Princess Anne above me. They helped me to my feet. I felt a huge lump on my head and had wrenched a muscle in my back. The pain was excruciating.'

Two years after Chipper's demise, with Dr Mugford's advice clearly ignored, the Queen was badly bitten and needed three stitches in her hand as she tried to break up a fight among her corgis at Windsor Castle. The Queen Mother's chauffeur John Collins, who tried to help, was also savaged and taken to hospital for a tetanus injection.

And in January 1994 Ranger, the killer, was at it again! This time he led a seven-strong pack as they tore into Fergie's Warwickshire terrier Bendicks at Sandringham. The victim – named after the Duchess of York's favourite chocolates – was rushed to an animal hospital where it needed 17 stitches to stem the flow of blood. Prince Andrew was so annoyed with the servant who allowed the dogs near each other that at first he wanted him sacked, but he eventually calmed down as Bendicks recovered.

Ironically, Bendicks survived only to embark on his own reign of terror. In 1996 he attacked carpet fitter Gary Ganley, 33, as he worked at Sunninghill Park, Andy and Fergie's home near Windsor. The following year he bit maid Charlotte Briggs, 23, who had to take two weeks off work because of her injuries. When she returned to Buckingham Palace she soon resigned after the aggressive pet refused to let her into Andrew's apartments.

His third attack was on Andrew's equerry Major Lance Gerrard-Wright. He was lucky not to lose an eye as Bendicks bit his face and left him with injuries needing several stitches. Fortunately he recovered and the handsome officer went on to become a male model who married Swedish TV star Ulrika Jonsson, although the relationship ended in 2006.

With the protection of the royal matriarch, Ranger remained untouchable. The Queen Mum was so fond of him that when he developed severe back problems, which made his hind legs drag, she could not bear the thought of him being put down. So royal handymen built a special two-wheel cart,

which was harnessed to his rear to act as legs. He was given training to take corners without rolling over and learnt to avoid narrow gaps too small for his wheels. Staff inevitably dubbed him the 'Lame Ranger' and shouted 'Hi-ho, Ranger – away!' as he went 'walkies'.

At the time the Queen Mother, the oldest person in the world to undergo two hip replacement operations, was 96, and Ranger was 98 in human terms. The two were inseparable and died within weeks of each other in 2002, Her Majesty at the ripe old age of 101, and Ranger 17, in dog years!

Knowing that Ranger was on his last legs, the Queen gave her mother a corgi for her 100th birthday in 2000. The pup was born to the Queen's pet Emma and went back to the Queen after her mother's death.

There was more sadness in 2001 when the Queen's by now favourite, Kelpie, died, aged 17, on Elizabeth's 75th birthday. A vet had to be called and the heartbreaking decision to put the dog down was made by Her Majesty herself.

But all of these canine capers were totally over-shadowed by the extraordinary events of Christmas 2003 at Sandringham. As the whole royal family gathered at the Jacobean palace in Norfolk, the Queen was looking forward to the traditional festivities that she enjoys so much. She had personally made up stockings packed with goodies for her corgis, including biscuits, chocolate drops, cake, crackers and plastic penguins with no squeak. It had not been a good year for her, after two knee operations, and she was still walking with the aid of a stick after the second one at the start of December.

On Monday 22 December the Queen was upstairs as Princess Anne arrived with her English bull terriers Dotty and Florence. As the bell rang and a footman opened the door, six corgis raced down the main staircase like excited children to greet the new arrivals. Their barking agitated Anne's dogs and one of them immediately set upon Pharos, the Queen's oldest and most loved corgi. Growls and yelps echoed through the house as the corgi's hind legs were savaged, with one of them broken in three places.

The Queen struggled down in a lift, which had been installed a couple of years earlier for the Queen Mum, and she and Anne, together with several servants, tried to pull the dogs apart.

One insider said: 'It was an incredibly distressing sight. There was blood everywhere. The poor corgi was howling but there was nothing Her Majesty or the princess could do to get the terrier off. It sank its teeth in and shook the corgi around.'

Staff made an emergency call to vet Roger Harverson, who drove six miles from King's Lynn. He put Pharos under sedation but the next day his condition deteriorated and he was put down. The Queen was said to be 'absolutely devastated' at the loss of a beloved pet who was always at her feet.

But there was worse to come. As the incident made headlines around the world and led TV bulletins, Anne's dog Dotty was blamed for the attack, and not without reason. The previous year she had mauled two boys aged seven and twelve who had been riding their bicycles through Windsor Great Park. Anne and her second husband, naval officer Tim Laurence, had been walking three dogs through the park just two days after the Queen

Mother's death when Dotty ran 150 yards to jump at the victims, causing them to fall from their bikes. Both lads received hospital treatment for bites and Anne was charged under the Dangerous Dogs Act and forced to appear in court.

She became the first member of the royal family in modern times to acquire a criminal record when she pleaded guilty to letting Dotty run out of control, and was fined £500 and ordered to pay £250 compensation. Judge Penelope Hewitt spared Dotty, then three years old, but warned she might be destroyed if there was another attack.

Once again, Dr Mugford was called in to help. He quickly cured Dotty's obsession with bicycles by squirting a harmless gas at her every time she saw them, and concluded: 'She is a quick learner and there need be no risk of public concern.'

For the best part of a week Buckingham Palace allowed Dotty to take the blame for the death of Pharos, but then, on December 29, it announced that she was INNOCENT! Florence was in fact the culprit, after teeth marks were examined and an internal investigation concluded Dotty was not guilty.

Then came the extraordinary news that Florence had now attacked a long-serving maid at Sandringham, just five days after killing Pharos. Ruby Brooker, a 58-year-old mother-of-three, was savagely attacked in a sitting-room as she finished her cleaning duties, and was left with blood pouring from her leg. Despite personal apologies from the

Queen and Anne, Ruby, who received hospital treatment for two bites above the knee, quit her job after 18 years' loyal service.

Had Florence really been responsible for both attacks – or was there a royal cover-up to prevent Dotty being destroyed? The truth may never be known, but the following year both dogs were back at Sandringham for Christmas, although, this time, they were kept in their rooms.

Servants only braved going into Anne's bedroom in packs of four. One insider said: 'The only way they felt safe was to shuffle in like Roman soldiers with tea trays as protection.'

By Christmas 2005 both dogs had been banished to sleep in Anne's Range Rover after the Queen refused to let them inside. But Anne was never going to change her ways and after the death of her third and older dog Eglantyne, she acquired yet another English bull terrier.

As for the Queen, Susan's line just goes on and on. In 2004 corgi pups Holly and Willow were born and kept by Her Majesty. She always tries to be present when one of her corgis gives birth, and each bitch is allowed one litter. Puppies are never sold, but those that are not kept are given to good homes.

The Queen spends so much time with her corgis that if she comes into the room wearing a headscarf, the dogs bound about excitedly, knowing they are going for a walk. But if she is wearing a tiara, they know she is heading for a banquet to which they are not invited. Quite simply she won't have a word said against them.

The late Sir Nigel Hawthorne, who played Machiavellian civil servant Sir Humphrey Appleby in the TV series *Yes Minister*, once told how he was 'terrified' at being invited to lunch at Buckingham Palace. But his discomfort was nothing compared to fellow guest Steve Davis, the snooker champion, who dared to make a joke about the dogs.

Sir Nigel recalled: 'I was talking to Steve when suddenly the door opened and in came the corgis followed by the Queen. We started having a conversation but Steve felt left out and the Queen was in mid sentence when he pointed at one of the corgis and said, "Is that the spoilt one?" The Queen was clearly very annoyed by this and said, "What do you mean by spoilt?" Steve replied, "You know, overfed." At this stage she looked really cross and said, "Corgis have small legs and they all look like that!" and then she turned away and charged off.'

On one occasion a footman carried a tray laden with tea and biscuits into the Queen's sitting-room when he became entangled with two corgis. They nipped at his ankles and finally caused him to fall, dropping the tray as he did. A large man, he fell heavily, twisting his leg. But when the Queen ran over she ignored him and fussed over the dogs! He limped out of the room without tea or sympathy and when he told his colleagues one laughed and said: 'What did you expect? We're just part of the furniture around here.'

The Queen hates anyone stroking her dogs to ingratiate themselves with her, and is indifferent to anyone who is attacked. In 2005 one of her favourite dressmakers, German designer Karl-Ludwig Rehse, told how he became a victim.

'I was having tea with the Queen when I realised I'd left my tailor's yardstick in one of the state rooms,' he said. 'There were six or seven corgis waiting to be fed and I made the mistake of running down the corridor. One of them bit me and I looked down to see a small hole in my trousers and a trickle of blood. But when I went back to the Queen I felt obliged to apologise for my dishevelled appearance and I ended up saying, "I'm very sorry, Your Majesty, but one of them bit me!"'

The Queen likes to feed her pets personally. A footman will bring her dishes of cooked meats, biscuits and gravy, which she mixes up herself and presents to them in silver bowls. For afternoon tea they will often be fed scones, or small biscuits shaped like Hovis bread loaves. A family joke is to watch bemused guests take a nibble from a biscuit only to be told, 'No, no, they're for the dogs!'

At Balmoral Her Majesty has sometimes instructed staff to reward corgis that catch rabbits by letting them eat the bunnies themselves!

At Sandringham Christmas puddings and cakes have often disappeared if left for a few minutes in the corgis' sight.

It is well known that the Queen is a believer in alternative medicine and homoeopathic cures, and this even extends to her dogs. A former footman revealed: 'One weekend at Windsor she told me that her dog Smokey was limping. We got some old pillow cases and tore them up into strips. Then she told me to hold Smokey on his back. So there

we were, the Queen and I, both down on our hands and knees. She rubbed some of her own cream in and then bandaged up the paw as if it was a sock on the end. She did it perfectly and within two or three days the paw had healed and Smokey was as good as new. She said if it was good enough for her, it was good enough for the dogs. It was a side of the Queen that not many people see.'

When Princess Michael of Kent once told a TV interviewer that she would like to shoot the Queen's corgis, the monarch reportedly told a friend: 'They are better behaved than she is!'

Her Majesty is so well known for her love of corgis that it's often forgotten how many other dogs she has had, all of which end their days in the pet cemetery at Sandringham. There have been numerous gundogs, Labradors and cocker spaniels. She and Prince Philip have had so many dogs throughout their marriage that it has been a task to find names for them all! The Duke once christened a litter Fiesta, Lagonda, Minx and Minor after British cars because the mother was called Mini. He named another set of black Labradors after hats – Trilby, Cap, Stetson, Bonnet and Turban. And a third bunch had names beginning with D – Drum, Dilys, Drama and Dolphin. The Queen also had two springer spaniels called Oxo and Bisto.

Like Princess Anne, Prince Charles inherited his parents' love of dogs but has also suffered the grief of losing them. The pet-loving British were astonished by a revelation in Jonathan Dimbleby's 1994 book on Charles that Diana made him get rid of his Labrador Harvey because the relationship made her jealous.

If Harvey could talk he would doubtless have been signed up by a newspaper for the tales he could tell. He was at Charles's side when he dated a string of girlfriends in the late 70s, including Lady Jane Wellesley, daughter of the Duke of Wellington.

Once, while at the Quorn Hunt, the playful pooch pushed the heir to the throne into a bush! But that didn't stop Charles from proudly posing with the dog at Balmoral for an official 30th birthday photo.

The demand for Harvey to go – since vehemently denied by some of Diana's friends – was made two years into their ill-fated marriage. According to Dimbleby, Charles reluctantly agreed to let him go 'to a good home in the country' where he died four years later.

When Charles and Diana's marriage began to crumble in the mid-1980s, the Prince was comforted by his Jack Russell terrier Tigga. In 1994 he was heartbroken when Tigga's daughter Pooh wandered off at Balmoral – and was never seen again. Charles even offered a reward in the local newspaper, but the dog probably fell down a rabbit hole. The Prince spent several days looking for Pooh and was apparently grief-stricken. He even stayed out all night with a torch, digging around with his bare hands and calling out for the pet.

The Queen Mother's former equerry, Major Colin Burgess, told how Charles, for some time afterwards, would suddenly become distant as he thought of the dog, trapped in a hole, slowly starving to death.

Everyone was sympathetic, but the Queen Mum, who had experienced the horrors of two world wars, simply said: 'Oh, I'm sorry to hear that. Anyway, have some tea.'

Whenever the Queen feels down, her immediate solution is always the same – a long stroll in the fresh air with her dogs to 'clear my mind'. There were many such walks at Balmoral in the week between Diana's death and funeral in 1997, as so superbly portrayed in the recent hit film *The Queen*, starring Helen Mirren. The royals will always have dogs because they are loyal, obedient and above all, trustworthy.

As the former Crown Equerry, the late Sir John Miller, once said: 'Like myself, Her Majesty prefers dogs to human beings. For one thing they don't talk so much!'

Servants: Upstairs and Sometimes Down the Stairs!

'Alcohol has played a major role in some extraordinary incidents involving servants at all of the royal palaces.'

A royal servant who was cycling to work through the grounds of Windsor Great Park one day in the 1980s came across what he thought was a member of the public bending under the bonnet of her broken-down car.

'Nice arse!' he cheekily observed.

'Thank you very much,' said Princess Anne, as she stood up to greet the red-faced admirer.

His luck was in as the Queen's only daughter saw the funny side. On a different day and in another mood, Anne can turn on her staff in a vicious manner, such as the time she blasted her chauffeur, using 'every swear word under the sun' when he arrived two minutes late.

The royals have always had a delicate love–hate relationship with their staff. Some become closer to their servants than they are to members of their own family. But despite years of loyal devotion, some flunkies can make one mistake at the wrong moment and find they are booted out of Buckingham Palace, never to return. The Queen, however, is generally tolerant when footmen or housemaids misbehave, because the old cliché 'you can't get the staff' is so true, and also because she becomes genuinely fond of some characters.

For years a large percentage of the 500 or so servants were gay, although the figure was probably never more than a third. With fewer family ties, they seemed to flock to royal service, despite appalling pay and long hours. The Queen Mum called them her 'knitting brigade' and once famously called down to her pages: 'When you two old queens have stopped gossiping will one of you fetch this Queen a gin and tonic!'

Inevitably the personal lives of some servants, just like the royals themselves, find their way into the tabloids. Bouffant-haired William Tallon was the Queen Mum's favourite servant and devoted half a century to looking after her. But when the 'Page of the Backstairs' was plastered across a Sunday newspaper for entertaining a young rent boy in his grace and favour rooms, she forgave him and simply joked 'Silly Billy'.

In the early 1980s a group of servants was suspended from duty after a gay 'orgy' aboard the Royal Yacht *Britannia*, photographs of which were sent to a paper. After an internal investigation the culprits were allowed to keep their jobs, with one favourite being told by the Queen to 'lie low and if possible get married'. He did just that – and now has two adult sons.

For a couple of years after the scandal there was an unspoken policy not to hire homosexuals as senior courtiers became worried about a 'gay mafia' wielding too much power.

'When you two old queens have stopped gossiping will one of you fetch this Queen a gin and tonic!'

One ex-footman said: 'I was asked when I joined if I had a girlfriend. They definitely wanted to reduce the number of gays but slowly they crept back. Life was sometimes made difficult for heterosexuals who didn't fit in and didn't want to socialise with the gays, some of who went to sleazy bars and clubs. Then AIDS came on the scene and there were all sorts of stories about people with the disease coming into daily contact with the royals. You sometimes felt the gays wanted you to go in straight and come out bent.'

In May 1992 the *Sunday Mirror* revealed another gay orgy, this time at Buckingham Palace, involving three footmen. Yeoman of the Silver Pantry, Kevin Lomas, walked into an unlocked room on the top floor staff quarters to discover the trio in a large Victorian enamel bath. According to the tabloid, the footmen, all in their twenties, were massaging each other with bath oils, scrubbing each other with loofahs and indulging in sex acts. Although the 'rub-a-dub-dub, three men in a tub' incident was reported, no disciplinary action was taken after the men claimed they were washing each other's feet. Perhaps as a result of changing attitudes, one of them was later promoted to a job in the Palace press office.

Around this time Prince Edward's valet, Brian Osborne, left his wife Carolyn to move in with a male telephonist working on the Palace switchboard.

'The "rub-a-dub-dub, three men in a tub" incident...'

(He also hit the headlines in 1992 when he left Edward's bath running in his Buckingham Palace apartment, causing £15,000 worth of damage to rooms flooded below.)

Heterosexual staff have, of course, had their fair share of affairs, scandals and lurid headlines as well.

The Queen's dresser Angela Kelly has worked her way up from humble beginnings to become Her Majesty's closest female servant and confidante. A 54-year-old Catholic from Liverpool, whose father was a gatekeeper at the city's docks, she now lives in a splendid grace and favour house in Windsor and drives a Land Rover Freelander. The Queen once told her: 'We could be sisters' and has made Angela a Member of the Royal Victorian Order, a personal honour from the monarch. But just a few years ago Angela was found rolling around on the ground having a fight with a maid 20 years her junior. She accused Hannah Coullett of seeing her then boyfriend, Palace pastry chef Tony Ferrirole, who was married!

Royal protection officers had to pull the two women apart as they scrabbled noisily on the floor of the servants' entrance at Buckingham Palace. Ferrirole, whose marriage survived the scandal, later resigned and left royal service. His wife Sarah said: 'All I know about Angela Kelly is that she had an affair with my husband.'

The Queen, as ever with a servant she likes, turned a blind eye. But some of Angela's colleagues feel she has become too full of her own importance. In another incident which made press headlines, she 'went berserk' and threw a bag of rubbish over a woman in the catering department because her lunch arrived late. Angela may have a temper, but she has won international praise for transforming the Queen's wardrobe and improving her fashion sense.

The Queen's favourite male servant is her page, 49-year-old bachelor Paul Whybrew. Known as 'Big Paul' because he used to work alongside the smaller Paul Burrell, he has been at the Palace for 30 years and has formed an extraordinary bond with his employer.

'The Queen loves Paul and wants him to stay with her for life,' said one servant. 'She is spending more and more time at Windsor Castle and so has provided him with a magnificent house there to make sure he is near her. They are so close that she will often just ask him in to her living-room to watch television with her if she is on her own, and they will spend hours chatting. He knows more about her than anyone else, but he is a hundred per cent trustworthy and would never betray her.'

It was 6 feet 4 inch Paul who came to the rescue during one of the most extraordinary incidents of the Queen's long life. At 7.15am on the morning of 9 July 1982, he was walking the corgis in the grounds of Buckingham Palace when unemployed labourer Michael Fagan scaled the walls and entered the Queen's bedroom. As the 31-year-old schizophrenic began to tell his monarch about his family problems, she pushed the panic button by her bed but got no response. She then telephoned the switchboard but the operator thought it was another member of staff playing a joke and replied: 'Yes, dear, you're the Queen, we'll send someone up!'

Fagan smashed a large glass ashtray and threatened to slash his wrists as he sat on the end of the Queen's bed.

The story then goes that a maid entered the room and exclaimed: 'Bloody 'ell Ma'am, what's he doing here?' before raising the alarm. But for the first time it can be revealed that the true hero was Whybrew. He returned with the corgis and as the Queen called him in he saw Fagan and began talking to him. Paul offered him a drink and then, when his guard was down, manhandled him outside where a maid did fetch a policeman.

'Paul has always played down his role and is very modest about it,' said an ex-colleague. 'But he was very brave and it was another reason why the Queen is so close to him.'

Alcohol has played a major role in some extraordinary incidents involving servants at all of the royal palaces. For years a cheap bar at Buckingham

Palace meant that booze flowed freely, but some staff unfortunately lost control of their intake.

Travelling yeoman Frank Holland was forced to retire in the mid 1990s after a series of drink related blunders involving the royal luggage. 'He kept sticking the wrong coloured labels on the wrong bags, and suitcases and other luggage went astray,' said one colleague. 'Frank was a lovely guy and the Queen adored him but over the years his boozing got worse and worse and he had to call it a day when he reached sixty.'

In the most notorious incident he fell down some stairs at a glittering state banquet right in front of her. A witness commented: 'The Queen just walked down, stepped over him, and said: "Would someone please come and pick Frank up, I think he's a little under the weather!"'

On a tour to Russia in 1994 she found him almost unconscious at the bottom of some stairs on *Britannia* while it was moored in St Petersburg.

'He was lying on the deck and she had to call for help,' said an insider.

Under the careful scrutiny of the then Keeper of the Privy Purse, Sir Michael Peat, a whole raft of perks, which made working for the royals more bearable, were axed during the 1990s.

Until 1993 each servant working at a royal function with more than 50 guests was given two free miniature bottles of scotch or gin, or a small bottle of port. That 'bonus' was withdrawn, but staff were still allowed to 'finish up the dregs' of opened bottles left at the end of banquets.

'You can imagine some of the fine wines served up to visiting heads of state and other dignitaries,' said one ex-footman. 'We were allowed to knock them back as we cleared up or take them back to our rooms. There were some great impromptu parties late at night.'

The hard-drinking culture among staff continues today if the 2004 Christmas party was anything to go by. Two servants ended up in hospital and a third slept on a bench in the grounds of Buckingham Palace with his kilt round his ears! In amazing scenes at the state apartments, guests knocked back champagne, wine and spirits, together with food worth a total of £100,000.

The Queen, Prince Philip, the Duke of York, the Earl and Countess of Wessex, the Princess Royal and her second husband Tim Laurence joined in the celebrations. But by midnight one footman had collapsed with alcohol poisoning and another had fallen down stairs and been taken to hospital with a suspected broken ankle.

The royals ate in the Queen's dining-room while the staff and their guests – wives, girlfriends and gay partners – feasted on salmon terrine, chicken and vegetables, followed by fruit sponge and cream.

*'Several servants staggered from the party and were sick
in the Palace gardens.'*

As the Joe Loss band and disco started up in different rooms, the royals emerged to mingle with the staff and join in the fun.

'The royals dance with their favourites and it's a great atmosphere,' said an insider.

But as the boozing gathered pace, 30-year-old footman Paul Mesher collapsed in the Picture Gallery and a doctor was called.

'He was so drunk he couldn't walk or talk,' said the observer. 'An ambulance was called and he spent two days in hospital.'

An hour or so later Keith Griffiths, a senior staff dining-room assistant in his mid-fifties, fell down the stairs at the Grand Entrance to the apartments, and another ambulance was called.

As the bacchanalia continued into the early hours, several servants staggered from the party and were sick in the Palace gardens. Tipsy housemaids struggled to stand up in their high heels as they took to the dance floor. And the next morning a Scottish under-butler in the glass pantry was found lying on a wooden bench within the palace quadrangle with his kilt up round his head and his 'crown jewels' on full display!

'Goodness knows how he managed to stay out in the cold without anyone noticing him but he was just left to sleep it off,' said the source.

The Gillies' Balls at Balmoral in Scotland, begun by Queen Victoria, provide another opportunity for the royals and staff to mingle and let their hair down together. During her annual two-month stay on Deeside, the Queen holds two parties because the servants change over half way through the holiday. Around 260 guests gather in the ballroom for drinks and canapés at 8pm while the royals eat dinner separately.

At about 9.30pm the Queen and her family descend a large sweeping staircase at one end, and after their dramatic entrance join in the fun straight away. The dancing starts with an eightsome reel played by the Queen's Piper, estate pipers and others from the Royal Guard. This is always followed by a 'Paul Jones' and other dances accompanied by a Scottish country band. Everyone dresses up, the men in tartan kilts, and the women in ball-gowns with tartan sashes. Sometimes the Queen and Princess Anne will wear tiaras, as the Queen Mum did when she was alive.

A regular commented: 'The balls are one of the highlights of the year because everyone from the Queen down to the lowest servant mixes in and enjoys themselves. People really go for it and the booze is flowing. You will see the Queen dancing with a 20-year-old footman or Zara Phillips with a 60-year-old gamekeeper. It's almost as if the royals go out of their way to dance with the lowest members of staff, maybe someone who washes dishes. There are servants up from London, the permanent staff at Balmoral and estate workers like gillies and the cowman who tends the royal herd. Some locals are also invited.

'Every drink is available, including a massive selection of different Scotches. The reels are what make it and you get taught the basics so you can join in. During the dances you get whirled round and could end up standing next to the Queen. Princess Diana used to love the parties and was fantastic on the dance floor.

'Very little has changed since Victoria's day. The hard wooden floor echoes to the sound of the dancing, there are stags' heads, claymores and shields on the walls, as well as wonderful old paintings. No-one leaves before the Queen, who might stay until midnight or a bit later. Sometimes the royals wander off for a rest and then return for more. The younger ones stay until the early hours and sometimes get served an early breakfast at dawn before going to bed!'

The Queen also attends a fancy dress ball at Balmoral, and judges the servants' efforts. One year three chefs poked fun at Prince Philip by turning up as scrap metal merchants carrying the wreckage of a car crash just days after he had written off his Land Rover. They were carrying a steering wheel and a car door, and even had a number plate with the right registration.

One insider observed: 'The Queen said "that's a bit close to home" and for a moment it looked as though the lads had gone over the top. It was quite a serious crash and the Duke was lucky not to have been seriously hurt or even killed. But she must have seen the funny side eventually as she gave them third place out of twenty outfits she was judging. First prize went to two dining-room assistants dressed as a duck and a mushroom. Everyone picks mushrooms at Balmoral and the Queen loves duck.'

One year at Balmoral the Queen heard that romantic chef David Quick had gone down on bended knee to propose to groom Elizabeth Harpin at Queen Victoria's beloved beauty spot Albert's Cairn.

She was so delighted by the gesture that she invited the couple to Craigowan Lodge where she was staying and offered a toast. The happy couple were overjoyed and left clutching a bottle of champagne each, with the Queen's best wishes ringing in their ears.

David and Elizabeth, who looked after Prince Philip's horses, did marry, and moved into a grace and favour house at Windsor, but sadly the marriage later broke up.

The royals are among the most famous people in the world, but servants have to get used to stumbling across their familiar faces in the most bizarre and unexpected circumstances. Even experienced hands are surprised by how informal the Queen can be.

One footman couldn't believe his ears when Her Majesty lay on the floor and told him: 'Would you please pull my pants orf!' The incident happened in the mid 1980s at Wood Farm, a five-bedroom farmhouse on the Sandringham Estate. According to the servant: 'All the royals had been out pheasant shooting on a horrible rainy and cold day. They were all there – the Queen, Philip, Charles, Andrew and Edward. They had been shooting in the morning and then they had lunch in a sort of covered garage where the Queen Mum greeted them with drinks. Everyone was very wet and sticky from the shoot and the weather. The Queen was wearing green Hunter wellington boots and Barbour waterproof leggings.

'All of a sudden she got down on the hard stone floor, lay on her back and said to me, "Would you please help me, would you pull my pants off?" I suppose I was just the nearest person. I helped her off with her wellingtons and then the leggings, which she obviously called pants. Under those she was just wearing woollen thermals.

'There were about twenty people all taking their clothes off and there was me holding the Queen's feet up in the air! It was an amazing scene and one I'll never forget. The Queen was just totally matter of fact about it.'

Two housemaids at Sandringham were grateful that the Queen has such a good sense of humour. For several minutes, as they walked round the gardens, they chatted away in a voice like hers to let off steam. A colleague who witnessed what happened next reported: 'You can imagine their shock when they turned round and saw her standing there. She must have heard their impersonations of her but she just smiled and walked on. It's just her snooty voice that cracks you up – but everyone loves working for her and respects her.'

On a hot summer's day at Balmoral, a footman was walking the corgis when he heard a shrill scream of excitement.

'I've won, I've won,' the Queen shouted as she performed an impromptu jig of delight on the lawn before disappearing back inside. And the reason for her joy? England's cricketers had just won a test against Australia!

On another bright sunny morning at Balmoral, two hunky servants of the heterosexual variety had an encounter with Princess Diana that became the main subject of gossip for several weeks afterwards.

The year was 1986 and the only sound that could be heard was the rushing waters of the River Dee. A wild red deer quickened his pace and headed off into the heather when he came across the pair. The two dining-room assistants were keen fitness fanatics, and were stripped to the waist to go through their normal body-building exercises.

In half an hour, after a refreshing shower, they would be laying the tables for the Queen, Philip and the rest to enjoy their breakfast of kippers, kedgeree and scrambled eggs.

Suddenly the weightlifting workout was interrupted by a familiar female voice. 'Can I watch?' came the inquiry as the bronzed musclemen turned to see Diana standing by a tree.

'Good morning, Ma'am,' they spluttered, not knowing where to look.

'Please carry on – don't mind me,' she said, giggling.

The men, red-faced with embarrassment, resumed their routine. But it wasn't long before Diana, her sensational figure shown off in tight jeans, a white blouse and jumper, took the initiative. She was a young mum of two and had been married to Charles for five years, but as the world now knows, the relationship was already on the rocks. To the servants, however, she was still the Princess of Wales, an untouchable royal icon.

Slowly she walked towards them and said, 'My, you have got such big muscles!' It was like a corny scene from a cheap movie. But to their utter amazement she carried on flirting and proceeded to feel their bulging biceps. Still laughing, she rubbed her hands over their glistening bodies, patted their firm six-pack stomachs and told them: 'All this working out is really paying off.'

Before they could really believe what was happening, she was gone.

'See you later,' she said, and walked back through the woods to the castle. The pair, one in his twenties and the other his early thirties, stood for a few seconds and gazed at each other in astonishment.

'No-one will ever believe us,' said one, but the encounter soon became the talk of the castle.

Said one servant: 'At first we didn't believe them but over the years Diana's flirting became more and more common. The way she flickered her eyes, her body language, all the signs were there when she was around a handsome man and wanted a bit of fun.'

Prince Philip's sense of humour is never far from the surface when he is with the staff, and he enjoys their jokes.

Former head chef Peter Page was once walking his dog at Windsor Castle. Philip asked him why he called the terrier 'Hovis' as in the brown loaf.

He replied: 'Because he's a well-BREAD dog!'

The Duke couldn't stop laughing all morning.

Nerves can sometimes be fraught for young members of staff who come face to face with the royals for the first time.

One inexperienced footman dropped some peas and carrots in Princess Anne's lap as he was serving her dinner, but fortunately she was in one of her good moods.

Another servant knocked a trolley full of food onto the carpet at a concert for Prince Edward in Buckingham Palace by violinist Vanessa Mae.

On Christmas Day 2004 the Queen fell backwards and was luckily cushioned by two of her corgis when a hapless servant pulled her seat away! Junior footman Fraser Marlton-Thomas, 25, thought Her

Majesty was getting up to go to the buffet table when he pulled her chair back. But she was simply passing a pepper pot to a relative and when she sat down she found herself sprawling on the floor.

There was a moment's silence before everyone realised the Queen wasn't hurt, and then Prince Philip and the rest of the family burst out laughing. One servant commented: 'Even the Queen thought it was hilarious.'

While some servants are in awe of their masters, others virtually tell the royals what to do!

One such figure was the Duke of York's beloved valet Michael Perry, who was almost like a father to Andrew. When he died in 2001 the Prince was devastated, and a former servant described the extraordinary bond they developed over 35 years.

'Michael started out as the chamber floor footman in 1966 when Andrew was just six,' he said. 'He also looked after Prince Edward and Princess Anne. He would play with them for hours, fetch all their meals, and generally look after them. There is no doubt that at that age they saw more of him and their nannies than they did of their parents, who obviously had their duties to perform.

'Andrew grew up with Michael as almost a surrogate dad, and he became his valet when he was about twelve. He always called Andrew "Sunshine" and the name just stuck. He was the only person who could get away with calling a royal by such a familiar name. He never called Edward or Anne by their titles either, just their Christian names.

'Andrew liked him so much because he spoke to him like a normal person without any airs or graces.'

As the prince became a teenager, and then gained his 'Randy Andy' sobriquet, chasing a string of beautiful women in his twenties, Perry was there as the ultimate 'fixer'.

A keen motor-biker who always had the latest 1,000cc model, he would roar out of Buckingham Palace with Andrew on the back for secret liaisons with the American actress Koo Stark and other girlfriends.

'No-one recognised the Prince with a helmet on, and photographers didn't expect him to be on the back of Michael's bike as they weaved in and out of the London traffic,' said the ex-servant. He was able to have dozens of secret romantic meetings like that.'

No-one was more delighted than Perry when Andrew married Sarah Ferguson at Westminster Abbey in 1986, and the loyal servant was an honoured wedding guest. But when the marriage went wrong, it was Perry who provided Andrew's salvation by persuading him to take up golf.

'He had been on and on at him for years, telling him what a great game it was, but Andrew didn't want to know,' said one friend. 'But when Andrew and Sarah split, the Duke became very depressed and lazy. He was sitting around watching TV, blue videos and eating junk food, and it was Michael who finally snapped him out of it and got him out on the course.

'He was quite a good golfer himself, about a fourteen handicap, and he taught Andrew the basics. From then on they were golfing partners and they played hundreds of rounds as buddies. It brought them even closer together.'

A small, thin man, Perry never married, but the ex-colleague explained: 'He wasn't gay like so many servants at the palace. Michael had quite a few girlfriends but he was devoted to Andrew. Maybe he spent too much time looking after him at the expense of his own relationships. You couldn't get a more devoted servant. He was there for him twenty-four hours a day.'

Perry was the only person who could handle Andy and Fergie's vicious dog Bendicks. 'He loved the dog and the feeling was mutual,' said one servant.

When Perry wasn't up walking Bendicks as usual one morning in August 2001, police broke into his room and found the dog whimpering beside his body. He had suffered a heart attack and died aged 62.

Andrew, who had been at Balmoral, returned from Scotland for the funeral.

'It is no exaggeration to say that he was closer to Michael than almost anyone else – even his own parents,' said the source. 'Michael was an uncle figure, friend and confidant rolled into one, and the Duke misses him terribly.'

In recent years morale has been low among staff, whose pay, perks and pensions have been slashed. An influx of Poles was even considered to keep numbers up. But whatever their nationalities, the royals will always need a steady supply of servants to cater for their daily needs – and sometimes become lifelong friends as well.

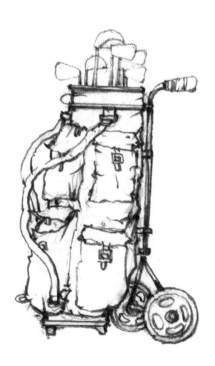

Royal Sneaks: Orf With Their Heads!

'The "unforgiven" – the servants and ex-members of the royal househald who write books or sell secrets to newspapers.'

They are the 'unforgiven' – the servants and ex-members of the royal household who write books or sell secrets to newspapers.

Once they have committed this cardinal sin, these 'traitors' are ostracised forever. The royals hate the fact that someone makes money out of them, just as much as the revelations that appear in the tabloids and magazines worldwide.

Above all they feel betrayed by aides they once trusted. But to some extent they only have themselves to blame. Staff wages are so poor that despite the Official Secrets Act and signed confidentiality agreements, many servants are still tempted to put pen to paper, sometimes with devastating results.

The royals call it 'doing a Crawfie' after the Queen's former governess Marion Crawford, who became the first royal sneak in 1950. By today's standards her account of a 16-year career bringing up the young 'Lilibet' and her sister Margaret was innocent stuff. But in a grey post-war world the public was crying out for fun and colour, and Crawfie's royal gossip fitted the bill on both sides of the Atlantic.

The Scottish nanny told how Elizabeth, who never went to school, liked to ride her like a horse. 'One of Lilibet's favourite games was to harness me with a pair of red reins that had bells on them, and off we'd go ... I would be patted, given my nosebag and jerked to a standstill.'

One day at Buckingham Palace with her 'little girls' she took a transatlantic call from the King and Queen: 'We ended the conversation by holding the Queen's corgi Dookie up, and making him bark down the telephone by pinching his behind.'

And in a fascinating insight into the Queen's mind at a young age, she recalled: 'I got quite anxious about her. She would hop out of bed several times a night to get her shoes quite straight, her clothes arranged just so.'

A year after leaving royal service in 1949, and egged on by her husband George Buthlay, Crawfie first sold her anecdotes to an American magazine, and then published *The Little Princesses*. She made more than £60,000, a fortune in those days, but it came at a price. The royals never spoke to her again and she was vilified in the press. She bought a house near the road from Aberdeen to Balmoral, and from her window could see the royal cars pass as they headed for their annual holiday on Deeside, but they never called in to see her.

After her husband's death in 1977, Crawfie became even more reclusive. Neighbours remembered her sitting by her fire looking through a box of mementoes – paintings and poems done by the princesses, and letters and Christmas cards. She even made a half-hearted suicide attempt, which her doctor called a 'cry for help'.

Shortly afterwards, in 1988, she died aged 79. Her 'treasure trove' of memories, including valuable photos, was worth thousands of pounds. But in her will she left the lot to the Queen, who placed them in the royal archive. It was, perhaps, Crawfie's way of saying 'sorry'.

Ironically, the book that so outraged the Palace

greatly boosted the popularity of the royal family. It is now almost an historical document, the only first hand account of the Queen's childhood.

From then on all staff had to sign a confidentiality agreement, but that didn't stop others following in Crawfie's footsteps.

Stephen Barry, Prince Charles's valet for twelve years, made £500,000 from two books in the early 1980s. The Palace claimed he had signed a secrecy agreement, but when challenged, were unable to produce it.

Barry, a flamboyant homosexual, was forced out in 1982 by Diana, who was shocked by his closeness to Charles. The final straw was his habit of coming into the newly-weds' bedroom early in the morning to open the curtains.

Barry's memoirs were bland and not vindictive, but they bought him apartments in California and London, where he indulged in a hedonistic lifestyle until his death from an AIDS-related illness in 1986. He was just 37.

John Barratt was a top royal aide for 20 years, a popular, handsome courtier who seemed happily married with two children. After his boss, Lord Mountbatten was murdered in 1979, Prince Charles got him a job with Prince and Princess Michael of Kent. But he fell out with Princess 'Pushy' and, after leaving his wife, moved to America. There he realised he was gay and began a series of sordid relationships with rent boys. Returning to London broke in the late 1980s, he decided to cash in and wrote a book called *With the Greatest Respect* in which he claimed Princess Michael rowed with Charles and Diana, went on wild shopping sprees and had a bizarre attitude towards her children.

It netted him £40,000 but by 1990 he was working as a £175-a-week road sweeper in London. Just three years later he was dead from AIDS at 59.

Malcolm Barker, former Clerk to the Royal Household, was paid £1 million in the early 1990s for a book called *Living with the Queen*. His tales of homosexual goings-on, drunkenness and theft at Buckingham Palace were published in America, but not in Britain after he was threatened with legal action. The book was also published in Canada under the somewhat less informative title of *Courting Disaster*. Barker also claimed that several bodies were buried under Buckingham Palace in 'suspect circumstances'.

Ex-Royal Marine Ken Stronach succeeded Stephen Barry as Charles's valet. He too worked for Lord Mountbatten, and Charles took him on in 1979 after the Earl's death. For 16 years he gave unblemished service, and seemed set to be the Prince's right-hand man for the rest of his career.

But moustachioed Stronach, who liked to dress like Charles in smart blue blazers, had a complicated private life and a violent streak. In 1994 his first wife Lillian told how he would regularly beat her up during their earlier marriage. In 1990 Stronach left his second wife Brenda after just 17 months for a 26-year-old Palace maid Diana Johnson, who later became his third wife.

Although he lived in a grace and favour house and had an expensive car, Stronach's salary was just £12,000 a year. Perhaps desperate for cash, he approached the *News of the World* to sell his story. He had also decided that Charles was a hypocrite, because the Prince had always asked his staff to keep quiet, but then confessed to adultery in his 1994 interview with Jonathan Dimbleby.

Stronach's story included claims that Charles and Camilla Parker Bowles made love in the bushes at the Prince's Highgrove home while Diana was asleep inside. He claimed one of his duties was to scrub grass stains from his master's pyjamas after the romps. During one heated row at Highgrove, Charles reputedly threw a heavy bootjack at Diana, which narrowly missed her. Stronach also sold pictures of the inside of Charles's bedroom.

But of all the sneaks, he probably suffered the most. He claimed he never got paid for his story, but was still forced to resign. Charles then took High Court action to stop him ever selling more secrets or writing a book.

Shortly after he lost his job aged 50 in 1995, his daughter Tracy, from his first marriage, claimed he had raped her during ten years of sexual abuse. Police did not press charges, but Stronach's life was in tatters and he disappeared into obscurity.

Wendy Berry was housekeeper at Highgrove from 1985 until 1993 and saw Charles and Diana's marriage crumble in front of her. She had signed a confidentiality agreement and so when in 1995 she wrote her book *The Housekeeper's Diary*, Charles took out a High Court injunction against her. She fled to America where she was paid an estimated £150,000 and the book was published. But she spent the next two or three years in Canada and Ireland, almost 'on the run', knowing that if she returned to Britain all profits could be seized.

The book gave detailed accounts of arguments between Charles and Diana. She also told how the Princess and army officer James Hewitt slept together at Highgrove while Charles was away.

In 2000 it emerged that Wendy had quietly slipped back into England and was living in Liverpool. After all the royal scandals and divorces of the 1990s, and Diana's tragic death in 1997, Charles decided to show clemency, and instructed his lawyers not to take any further action against Wendy. Now 75, she still lives on Merseyside and dotes on her grandchildren.

Patrick Jephson, now 51, worked for Princess Diana between 1988 and 1996, first as her equerry and then as private secretary. He resigned after her infamous *Panorama* interview, when she admitted adultery with James Hewitt and predicted that Charles would never be king.

The Cambridge graduate and former naval lieutenant commander always claimed to be a loyal servant. But in 2000 his book *Shadows of a Princess* caused a storm, portraying her as a cruel and scheming hypochondriac, who liked telling dirty jokes. Buckingham Palace condemned it and Prince William said: 'Harry and I are quite upset about it, that our mother's trust has been betrayed and that even now she is being exploited.'

Jephson had cleverly not signed a confidentiality agreement until shortly before his resignation, and made about £2 million from the book and its serialisation in the *Sunday. Times.*

He lost a lot of his profits in a costly divorce, but he is now married to the wealthy former White House aide Mary-Jo Jacobi. He wrote a second book, *Portraits of a Princess: Travels with Diana*, and continues to pontificate about the royal family in newspaper and magazine articles.

Paul Burrell is the world's most famous ex-royal servant and is now a millionaire celebrity in his own right. But just five years ago he was faced with financial ruin and a possible prison sentence.

Burrell, 50, would claim he is not a 'sneak' at all but the self-appointed guardian of Princess Diana's memory. He has made more than £4 million from books, newspaper interviews and TV appearances since Diana's death in 1997. But the public tired of him 'cashing in' long ago and he is often referred to as a 'traitor' in the popular press.

He arrived at Buckingham Palace as an 18-year-old in 1976 and within a year was appointed the Queen's personal footman. After ten years at her side he became Charles and Diana's butler in 1987, and when they split in 1992, stayed with the Princess.

Burrell claims Diana called him her 'rock' and 'the only man I can trust'. And when she died there is no doubt he was almost suicidal with grief. But when he became a fundraiser for the Diana, Princess of Wales Memorial Fund, members of the Spencer family considered he was getting above his station, and he was forced out of his job.

In January 2001 Burrell was arrested at his Cheshire home accused of stealing over 300 items belonging to Diana. Some estimates put the value of the clothes and other possessions as high as £5 million. Police were also looking for a mahogany box in which Diana kept intimate letters and other valuables, which became known as the 'Crown Jewels'.

Among the missing contents was a tape recording made by Diana of an interview she had with a former Palace servant George Smith. Smith had claimed he had been the victim of a homosexual rape by one of Prince Charles's servants in 1989. He reported the incident in 1996, but after a seven-month internal inquiry, nothing was done.

On 1 November 2002, after several days of evidence, Burrell walked free from the Old Bailey in London when his trial was dramatically halted. The court was told that the Queen had remembered a conversation two years earlier when Burrell told her he had taken Diana's possessions into 'safe keeping'. The case had collapsed, but cynics suggested the Queen's recollection had more to do with fears about what Burrell was going to say in open court about Smith's allegations and other scandals.

Burrell was now free to sell his story – and he did so to the *Daily Mirror* for £300,000. Other newspapers turned on him, however, with several running stories about his alleged homosexual past.

In 2003 Burrell wrote a book called *A Royal Duty*, which sold 300,000 copies worldwide and earned him a small fortune. His most sensational revelation was that Diana had written a letter ten months before her death, in which she predicted she would die in a car 'accident'.

Last year his second book *Diana: The Way we Were* flopped, selling just a few thousand copies.

Burrell has appeared on *I'm A Celebrity Get Me Out Of Here!* and as an adviser down under to a series called *Australian Princess*. He has even launched his own range of wine called the 'Royal Butler' collection. His career has bought him a £750,000 home in Cheshire and a holiday retreat in Florida, where he stays with his wife Maria, a former Palace maid, and their sons Alexander and Nicholas.

Food and Drink: Black Bananas and Teetotal Toasts

'Princess Anne will only eat bananas when their skins are totally black.'

Princess Anne will only eat bananas when their skins are totally black. The Queen doesn't like champagne and only pretends to sip it when proposing toasts. And Prince Andrew doesn't drink at all! These are some of the extraordinary facts to emerge about the royals' culinary likes and dislikes.

Certainly they have never had a reputation for being gourmets. Historian Sir Roy Strong, former Director of the National Portrait Gallery, was astonished by the poor quality of food he was served when he was invited to lunch or dinner with the Queen Mother at her London home, Clarence House. He said of one lunch in December 1977: 'The food was really bad. Deep fried rissoles, frozen Brussels sprouts and mashed potatoes, even if they are served on silver, don't rank in my running as even good plain food.'

Four years later things hadn't improved much. In April 1981 he recorded: 'The food was, as usual, indifferent. An over-decorated stodgy salmon mousse, meatballs, beans and potatoes, and an ice cream with black cherries.'

The Queen has inherited her mother's taste for plain, simple fare. She relishes home cooking because she has to attend so many official banquets when the food is often rich.

Her day starts when her personal maid takes her a pot of Earl Grey tea and a few Marie biscuits –

named after the Grand Duchess Marie of Russia, the wife of Prince Alfred, Queen Victoria's fourth son. (Prince Philip prefers black coffee and rarely drinks tea of any sort.)

Although she has a healthy appetite, Her Majesty doesn't indulge in a 'full English' breakfast any more, preferring toast, marmalade and tea, although much of her toast ends up with the corgis at her feet.

She might occasionally have some scrambled eggs, and, thanks to an undercover reporter from the *Daily Mirror* who spent two months working as a footman in 2003, we know that cereals and porridge oats are also on the breakfast table in plastic Tupperware containers, alongside a bowl of fruit.

Philip sometimes has a fry-up, and he also has a liking for oatcakes with honey.

'Little and often' is said by many to be a healthy way of eating, and the royals certainly believe in that maxim. The Queen's meals always consist of high quality food, but in small portions. She drinks still Malvern water throughout the day, often getting through two or three large bottles, and only drinks alcohol during the day on special occasions.

At Buckingham Palace the Queen often eats lunch alone. At around 1pm, after she has met visiting dignitaries, been answering letters or held an investiture, she will have a small piece of fish or chicken, accompanied by some fresh vegetables or salad.

Undoubtedly the royals' favourite meal is tea. Prince Charles once said the family was obsessed with it, and 'everything stops' for the afternoon ritual at 5pm. Dainty cucumber sandwiches with rounded edges cut to an exact size without crusts, homemade scones, potted shrimps, Dundee fruit cake and strong tea feature on a daily basis.

Former royal chef Graham Newbould, who, during a six-year stint worked for the Queen and Prince Charles, explained on a TV show *Secrets of the Royal Kitchen* in 2002: 'The royals never have square sandwiches because tradition has it that anyone presenting them with pointed-edged food is trying to overthrow the throne of England.'

For dinner the Queen loves traditional dishes like poached salmon, lamb cutlets, roast beef, duck *à l'orange*, and fish and chips. Her favourite is haddock fried in breadcrumbs, served with Béarnaise sauce and neat, thin French fries.

She and Philip don't normally have starters, but the Queen might have a cocktail before dinner, pink vermouth with soda or a gin Martini. Her husband prefers a beer, and Double Diamond used to be a favourite.

Despite access to some of the world's finest wines in the Palace cellars, the Queen normally favours a German Hock or a glass of Portuguese Mateus Rosé.

She has a sweet tooth and enjoys puddings like

chocolate mousse, poached pears, mint chocolate ice cream, summer pudding and lemon tart.

What every royal chef should definitely know is what NOT to serve Her Majesty. Garlic, onions, and tomato sauce are out, as are shellfish, curry and messy foods like spaghetti and other pastas with sauces.

Tomato pips and cucumber seeds have to be removed so as not to stick in her teeth, and soft fruits such as blackberries or raspberries are banned for the same reason. Chicken, game and fish are always boned for the benefit of guests and the royals. The fish bone that stuck in the Queen Mum's throat in 1986, requiring her to be airlifted 130 miles by helicopter from the Castle of Mey in the far north of Scotland to Aberdeen hospital, has never been forgotten.

Even at banquets the Queen likes to season her own food, and does not appreciate over zealous waiters wielding pepper mills.

But if she is hardly adventurous in her tastes, the Queen does enjoy one huge advantage over the rest of us when it comes to choosing fresh and wholesome ingredients. She has the pick of produce from her own homes – salmon and beef at Balmoral in Scotland; game and crabs from Sandringham in Norfolk; and lamb and vegetables from Home Farm, Windsor.

Prince Charles has taken an obsession with healthy eating to new levels. Wherever possible he will only eat food prepared by his own staff. Organic vegetables grown at Highgrove, his Gloucestershire home, are transported to him wherever he is. He even has them ferried 600 miles in trucks up to Balmoral, preferring his produce to that from the Queen's Scottish estate.

Carolyn Robb, the Prince's personal chef for eleven years, told how she was expected to take home grown food in 'piles and piles of cool-boxes' halfway round the world on official tours because Charles didn't want to risk local dishes.

Graham Newbould revealed the Prince's extraordinary breakfast requirements: freshly squeezed orange juice, a small bowl of freshly peeled and cut fruit, specially made muesli, milk from the Windsor Castle dairy, granary toast and SIX different types of honey!

Even Charles's great friend Deborah, Duchess of Devonshire, muttered 'how rude' when the Prince once stayed with her at Chatsworth House and brought his own grub.

The chef at Chatsworth, one of England's great stately homes, revealed Charles's demands for the 'perfect' picnic sandwich. French-born Hervé Marchand, who left his job after four years, had to contact the Prince's chef for instructions. 'Charles wanted a homemade organic granary bap exactly eight centimetres in diameter, and cut in half,' he said. 'I was told I had to cut it exactly to size if it were too big or small. I would butter the first half with mayonnaise, add pesto, shredded salad leaves and an egg, which had been fried on both sides so that it was not runny. I would then have to season the eggs and add two thin slices of Gruyère cheese.'

Marchand was then told he had to carefully butter the second half and smear a little Marmite on it, before placing the two halves together. But Charles still wasn't finished. He insisted the sandwich looked 'rustic', so the chef then had to cover it with a little white flour.

Charles's favourite supper dishes include: soft-boiled eggs with porcini mushrooms; crispy potato skins with spinach; and risotto with mushrooms picked from the Balmoral estate. (He once invited Italian restaurateur Antonio Carluccio to spend three days with him at the Deeside castle, showing him which wild mushrooms were fit to eat and which were poisonous.)

The Prince enjoys game pie made from whatever animals he or his sons have shot, and of course any salmon they have caught from the river.

He is not keen on desserts, preferring fresh fruit from his garden.

The Princess Royal is a lover of simple food, and has been seen tucking into a big plate of chips covered in tomato sauce on skiing holidays. She hardly touches alcohol, hates avocados, and drinks lots of Coca-Cola on foreign trips, claiming the American soft drink 'kills all known germs'.

But Anne also has one of the most bizarre cravings among her family. She adores bananas when they are over-ripe and the skins have turned black. When most people would be throwing the fruit onto the compost, Anne thinks they are delicious, and she also likes kiwi fruit when they are past their best and going soft.

Amazingly for a former naval officer, the Duke of York hates the taste of booze and never touches a drop. But he does have a weakness for sweets, particularly steamed syrup sponge, spotted dick and jam roly-poly.

Andrew has often struggled with his weight, and his penchant for puddings once earned him the sobriquet 'Duke of Pork' as he piled on the pounds.

Prince Edward loves chicken curry so much that he once asked for it almost every day for a month.

Anne, Andrew and Edward still have their own apartments at Buckingham Palace, but never eat together, and only rarely with their parents when they are staying in London. Despite being one of the richest women in the world, the Queen is renowned for her frugality and insists that all leftovers from meals are eaten the next day.

So, on Mondays, after a Sunday roast, she will often be eating similar meals to her servants – shepherd's pie, cottage pie, rissoles or a royal favourite, bubble and squeak. During one economy drive she substituted expensive champagne normally used at banquets with Tesco's own supermarket brand because 'who can tell the difference when it is served wrapped in white cloth?'

The Queen even gets her fine wines for entertaining on the cheap. Visiting heads of state and other VIPs quaff rare vintages worth thousands of pounds, not knowing they were bought for a fraction of their true value. Under a long-standing agreement, Buckingham Palace buys wines from the Foreign Office cellars at Lancaster House, but only for the price they cost decades ago.

The Queen Mother's capacity for alcohol has passed into royal legend and she once told a friend: 'It seems to have no effect on me whatsoever.'

On a walkabout in London's East End she once popped into a pub and downed a pint of bitter in front of astonished locals. But on a normal day she would begin with a gin and Dubonnet before lunch, followed by wine or champagne with the meal.

Her former equerry Major Colin Burgess recalled her drinking vast amounts of hard liquor, even though she was in her mid-nineties! In his 2006 book *Behind Palace Doors*, he claimed she drank claret and even port at lunch, and then at 6pm, her 'magic hour', she would tackle a large gin and tonic, followed by more champagne with her dinner.

Burgess told how, on a summer's day in 1995 in the garden at Clarence House, he had lunch with the Queen Mother, her elderly treasurer Sir Ralph Anstruther, her private secretary Sir Alistair Aird and her senior lady-in-waiting Dame Frances Campbell-Preston.

After a meal of an egg starter followed by chicken and mashed potatoes, he recalled: 'The wine, a full-bodied claret that wasn't really conducive to a hot summer's day, had been passed round and a few bottles drunk.'

Halfway through a conversation about the Second World War, all four of Burgess's companions fell asleep at the table, and remained there snoring for 35 minutes. 'Eventually I rang the bell for a servant to clear the plates, and blimey, as soon as it rang they all sat up and just carried on from where they had left off with Ralph exclaiming: "And of course the Italians simply gave in once the Germans had gone."'

In July 1989 Ashley Walton covered the Queen Mum's last tour of her beloved Canada. At an afternoon tea party for the smart ladies of Ontario, the royal matriarch was in fine form, strolling round the room and meeting dozens of admirers.

'She had a bone china cup and saucer, but I soon realised it wasn't tea she was drinking,' he said. 'She was being topped up with champagne by a member of her staff round the back. No wonder she was always in such a good mood!'

A conservative estimate puts the number of alcoholic units consumed by the Queen Mum at 70 a week, when health experts say 14 is the recommended 'safe' limit. But that didn't stop her living until the ripe old age of 101!

Although the Queen's sister Princess Margaret drank as much as her mother, she didn't always handle it as well. Famous Grouse whisky was her favourite tipple, and footmen were told to keep her cut glass tumbler constantly topped up.

In the mid-1980s *Daily Express* reporter Walton received an anonymous call suggesting he should cover a visit by Margaret to a British Army base at Hanover in Germany.

He was rewarded with the sight of a very drunk Princess literally falling out of an official car into the snow as she arrived for a ceremonial dinner in the officers' mess. As Margaret, the regimental Colonel-in-Chief, was helped to her feet, a photo was taken and appeared the next day in the *Express* under the headline: 'Princess Margaret is unwell'.

The truth was that at that time, Margaret, who was divorced from Lord Snowdon in 1978, was drinking even more than usual to drown her sorrows over the end of her romance with younger lover Roddy Llewellyn.

Years of heavy drinking and smoking caught up

with her and she died aged 71 in February 2002. Incredibly, the Queen Mother, who was 101 and suffering from a heavy cold, attended her daughter's funeral, but then passed away a few weeks later.

The Duchess of York enjoys a drink or two. Laurent-Perrier pink champagne is a particular favourite.

In 1987, just a year into her ill-fated marriage to Andrew, she took him on a two-day trip to some of the world's greatest wine cellars in France. While Sarah sampled some of the best wines of the Medoc, Andrew stood sipping mineral water and looked decidedly fed up.

British Consul Dennis Amy said: 'Everyone was puzzled that a member of the royal family who does not drink accepted such an invitation.'

After a heavy dinner accompanied by the finest vintages of the prestigious Chateau Beychevelle, an angry looking Andrew was seen literally dragging a very merry Duchess up an outside staircase into their bedroom for the night.

Prince Charles is partial to most alcohol, but never to excess. He loves Laphroaig malt, and even has a special Highgrove edition of the whisky from Islay on sale in his Gloucestershire estate shop.

The subject of drinking, though, is one of Charles's favourite conversation pieces. Whenever he meets members of the public on walkabouts, boozing is never far from his lips.

'Do you have a good drink up after work?' is a typical question.

He once told an Irishman he met in England: 'I'd love to go to Ireland and have a pint of Guinness, but they might blow me up or something!'

And in a market in Budapest, Hungary, he asked bewildered stall-holders: 'Do you like chasers with your beer?'

The Queen frowns upon smoking, having seen her father George VI die young from lung cancer.

Prince Philip gave up the habit on the eve of his marriage as a 'wedding gift' to his beautiful young princess.

Prince William only has a cigarette occasionally but brother Harry puffs through 20 a day when he is not under the eye of senior officers in the army.

Both the princes, along with Charles's second wife Camilla, Duchess of Cornwall, are trying to give up the weed.

The royals have been treated to sumptuous feasts prepared by some of the world's top chefs on their travels. But they have also had to eat some hideous traditional dishes so as not to offend their hosts. Rats, slugs and sheep's heads complete with staring eyes have been among the 'delicacies' they would rather have declined.

The Queen was served rat stew when she visited the Central American state of Belize, and afterwards said that it tasted like rabbit. In fact it was a dibnut, similar to a large chipmunk. The rodent is still a firm favourite in Belize restaurants where it is billed as 'Royal Rat' or 'Rat eaten by Her Majesty Queen Liz'.

On an historic tour of China in 1986, the Queen was presented with a sea slug, a purple, slimy specimen about three inches long. But unlike the hapless contestants of bush-tucker trials in the TV show *I'm A Celebrity Get Me Out Of Here!* the ever professional monarch was prepared. She had been warned about some of the dishes that would be served up at the banquet in the Great Hall of the People in Beijing's Tiananmen Square, and she had spent hours at Buckingham Palace learning how to use chopsticks.

The sea cucumber, or echinoderm, arrived in a sealed brown earthenware pot. All eyes were on her as she delicately lifted the lid, and, using her ivory chopsticks, poked around inside. She lifted the slippery morsel to her mouth and down it went, without a change of expression.

'Delicious,' she said, turning to her hosts.

It was a brave display, unlike an aide who pretended to drop the slug on the floor, and claimed she couldn't find it under the table. Later Her Majesty said it was a bit like shrimp, and her verdict on shark's fin soup was that it 'tasted of not much'.

On a visit to the exotic South Sea island of Tonga, the Queen followed the local custom of eating roast suckling pig with her fingers, nervously pulling pieces from the animal, which still had its head and tail.

Prince Charles, on his first ever tour of India, ate everything that was set before him. He knew he would suffer from 'Delhi belly' and tried to take precautions, a broad based antibiotic, before the trip. But he told High Commission staff it hadn't worked, adding: 'I spent a lot of time in the lavatory. It was like walking on egg shells.'

On a visit to Kyrgyzstan he picked up a sheep's head and later said: 'The eyes were staring back at me!'

Whatever their different tastes, the modern day royals seem a healthy bunch, and are a testament to the old saying: 'You are what you eat.'

Horses: Equestrian Affairs

'Ask any member of the royal household if the Monarch likes a punt and the reply is always: "Of course not!"'

The Queen and the late Queen Mother have had more than 1,000 winners between them as racehorse owners, but of course Her Majesty never bets herself – or does she? Ask any member of the royal household if the monarch likes a punt and the reply is always: 'of course not!'

But the co-author of this book, Ashley Walton, begs to differ.

The Queen was a regular at the Badminton Horse Trials in Gloucestershire in the early 1980s, and would often wander unrecognised among the public in headscarf and tweeds.

One Saturday morning Walton, then working for the *Daily Express*, took up a position on top of a farm vehicle armed with a powerful pair of binoculars. It wasn't long before the Queen emerged from her private marquee beside Badminton House with her loyal aide, the Crown Equerry Lieutenant-Colonel Sir John Miller. Sir John was in charge of the Queen's horses, carriages and cars, and he and the Queen were soon studying the form guide in that morning's *Sporting Life*, the racing newspaper.

The Queen used a pen to highlight a runner and a decision was clearly made. Sir John strode off purposely, across the showground, past the competitors' ring and burger vans, and straight into the Ladbrokes betting tent. The nationwide chain of bookmakers was an established part of the Badminton scene, taking bets on the event and other meetings throughout the country. Our

enterprising reporter followed Sir John and stood behind him as he wrote out a betting slip and handed £50 to the cashier. As Sir John turned round, clutching his slip, the two came face to face.

'Good morning, sir. Is that a bet for Her Majesty?' asked Walton, coming straight to the point.

Sir John, described in his *Daily Telegraph* obituary on 20 May 2006 as 'effortlessly polite and wholly devoted to his sovereign, although he was rather less genial to those whose social position was unclear to him', went puce, spluttered with indignation, and snarled: 'How dare you, sir.'

He then stormed back to the royal tent. There he could be seen giving the betting slip to the Queen, before pointing out to her the man with the binoculars, and obviously telling her what had happened.

'The Queen watched me for a couple of seconds, almost in disbelief, and then went back inside, still clutching the slip,' said Walton. 'I'm sure she loves to put cash bets on just like everyday punters, but obviously she does it through a third party.'

For years there had been rumours that the Queen Mum had a telephone account with the same bookies. Intrepid hack Hugh Whittow, of the *Daily Star*, was desperate to find out if it was true. And one year, at the Epsom Derby meeting, he saw his chance. In those days – the early 1980s – it was frowned upon to actually talk to the royals directly. But that didn't deter Whittow, who was unimpressed by such protocol. He was sitting in the grandstand press box, right next to the royal box. From this privileged spot, journalists could see into the private world of royal racing, witnessing the excitement or despair as the Queen or Queen Mum's horses won or lost.

The Queen Mum was right there, leaning against a small glass screen, with a glass of champagne in her hand. She was just a few feet away from Whittow, and as she looked across, she smiled and wished him a cheery 'good morning'.

Hugh, fortified by a couple of drinks himself, took this as an invitation. 'Tell me, Ma'am,' he said in his lilting Welsh accent, 'do you bet on the horses yourself?'

The Queen Mum, always a good sport, laughed and replied: 'You can't ask that!' But she didn't move, and Whittow was about to continue the conversation when the Queen appeared at her mother's elbow and guided her away. The look that Her Majesty gave him could be politely described as hostile.

The next year the small glass screen separating the royals from the 'reptiles' had been replaced with a big frosted glass barrier complete with plastic shutters on the royal side.

Whittow's cheek didn't ruin his career – he is now deputy editor of the *Daily Express*. Racing has given the Queen and the Queen Mother enormous pleasure over the years, but also a fair share of tragedy and heartache. Her Majesty has had more than 600 winners in 58 years as an owner, nearly all of them on the flat, while the Queen Mother had more than 450 winners before her death in 2002, mostly over the jumps in National Hunt racing.

In 1949 a horse called Monaveen, jointly owned by the royal pair, won over the fences but had to be destroyed after breaking a leg the following year in a race at Hurst Park. The then Princess Elizabeth was so upset she turned her attentions to the flat, which she regarded as far less dangerous, and didn't have another jump win for 53 years when First Love won at Folkestone in February 2003.

The Queen's resolve had weakened because of her mother's death the previous year. And she decided to honour her memory, and the affection with which she was held in National Hunt circles, by racing her best young jumpers in the sovereign's colours of purple, gold braid, scarlet sleeves and black velvet cap.

The Queen Mother read the *Sporting Life* every day, often before *The Times* or *The Daily Telegraph*, and racing became a passion for her after she was widowed.

Her horse Devon Loch suffered one of the most dramatic defeats in racing history when he looked to have the 1956 Grand National in the bag. Just 100 yards from home he jumped an imaginary fence and sprawled on the ground. The crowd was aghast, and the grainy black and white TV pictures of the extraordinary moment have passed into racing history. But the Queen Mum just smiled gracefully and the next day sent a cigarette box to the horse's trainer Peter Cazalet, as a memento of a 'terrible yet glorious day'.

In 1952, on the death of her father George VI, the Queen inherited the royal stud at Sandringham and has spent about half a million pounds a year in today's terms on her hobby ever since. She currently has around 25 horses, the progeny of about 18 mares kept in Norfolk. But although she is normally in the top 20 of owners each year, she struggles these days to compete with modern giants of the turf like the Maktoum family of the United Arab Emirates or the Coolmore Stud in Ireland.

For 33 years Her Majesty's racing manager was her best male friend, the seventh Earl of Carnarvon, grandson of the fifth Earl who discovered Tutankhamen's tomb in 1922. They met as teenagers and when she was 17, they famously danced together at a London debutantes' ball.

After the war, Carnarvon, then Henry Herbert, frequently escorted Princess Elizabeth to the races, and their relationship deepened. The Queen called him 'Porchie' after his then courtesy title Lord Porchester, and the nickname stuck even after he succeeded his father as Earl in 1987. Carnarvon became the Queen's racing manager in 1969 and he called her almost daily from his family seat, Highclere Castle in Hampshire, and she was a frequent visitor to the stud there.

Although Carnarvon was happily married to American Jean Wallop, he and the Queen were so close that it has often been suggested their friendship bordered on the romantic.

One servant recalled: 'Whenever she took a call

from him her face would light up. It was always one of the highlights of the day for her.'

The Queen's horse Highclere won the 1,000 Guineas in 1974. And three years later another, Dunfermline, won the Oaks and St Leger in the same season. But sadly, Carnarvon's career will always be remembered for two appalling blunders. The Queen has never achieved her greatest racing ambition, to win the Derby, and Carnarvon must take some of the blame.

In 1982 he advised her to sell Height of Fashion for £1.5 million to Sheik Hamdan bin Rashid Al Maktoum. It was a good price, and the money was used to buy stables at West Ilsley in Berkshire, where her principal trainer Major Dick Hern became based. But Height of Fashion went on to breed Nashwan, which won the Derby and the 2,000 Guineas in 1989, and Carnarvon had clearly made a mistake in selling the young horse.

The second blunder was much worse though, and was once described as 'the saddest, nastiest episode in racing history'. In 1984 the immensely popular Hern, known to all in racing as The Major, broke his neck in a hunting accident. He was confined to a wheelchair but was still able to continue training to a very high standard. But in 1988, while Hern was in hospital for a heart ailment, Carnarvon told the Major's wife Sheilah that his lease on the stables at West Ilsley would not be renewed, in effect sacking him as the Queen's principal trainer. Hern was given just two weeks to get out and the world of racing was shocked to the core. Even the Queen Mother and Princess Anne told the Queen the decision was wrong.

Former royal jockey Willie Carson said Anne was 'livid' and the Queen Mum was said to be 'outraged'.

The shabby treatment of Hern caused such uproar in racing circles that there were fears for the Queen's good name. Ian Balding, at the time the Queen's other trainer and the man who conceivably had most to gain from Hern's sacking, also backed his colleague. He told the Queen's private secretary Sir Robert Fellowes: 'If you don't make some sort of arrangement for Dick Hern, it will be the most unpopular thing the Queen has ever done and she risks having her horses booed in the winners' enclosure. That's how strongly people in racing feel and I think she should know that.'

When Nashwan, trained by Hern, won the 2,000 Guineas in May, 1989, the roar of applause in the winners' enclosure was said by racing correspondents to be the nearest thing they had ever witnessed to a display of anti-royalist feeling.

The Queen and Carnarvon were not there to hear it, but Her Majesty did meet Hern after the horse then won the Derby. Their conversation that day has always remained a secret.

Stung by the criticism, the Queen allowed Hern to stay in the rectory that had been his home since 1962, and he was given a year's grace at West Ilsley.

He was saved from premature retirement when Sheik Hamdan bin Rashid Al Maktoum provided him with new stables, and he worked for another seven years.

The Herns and the Carnarvons had been friends, even going on holiday together, but they never got over the row. Carnarvon blamed the sacking on two doctors who said The Major wasn't well enough to work. He said: 'I was responsible entirely for one thing, and that was the management of the stable by someone who was fit and capable of running it properly.'

But it later emerged that Carnarvon had previously ignored the advice of three other doctors who said Hern would recover enough to carry on.

In 2000 The Major broke his silence and gave an interview to mark the publication of his authorised biography. He said: 'The Queen was badly advised. It was a very un-British practice of kicking a man when he was down. Carnarvon panicked because he thought I was going to die and the stables would be left without a trainer. What really riled me was that instead of coming to see me in hospital, and looking me in the eye, he summoned my wife.'

Soon after the fracas, Sheilah Hern learnt she had cancer of the intestine, and The Major was convinced the stress of the fight was a contributory factor. After six major operations, she died in 1998.

On 11 September 2001 the world was shocked by the terror attacks in America, when hijacked aircraft were flown into New York's Twin Towers and the Pentagon in Washington. But as the Queen sat, glued like millions of others to the television, she received a call to say that her beloved 'Porchie' had died that day aged 77 of a heart attack.

Three days later she attended a remembrance service in St Paul's Cathedral for the victims of the atrocities. As she emerged from the moving event into the warm autumn air of London, her eyes were red and tearful. Few knew that as well as mourning the deaths of hundreds of innocent people, she was also weeping for the loss of her dearest friend. The Queen rarely attends funerals, but she went to Carnarvon's, again demonstrating her deep affection for him.

Major Hern, who was awarded a CBE in 1998, died aged 81 the following year. In the early 1980s Prince Andrew dated Carnarvon's beautiful daughter, Lady Carolyn Herbert. But the relationship soon fizzled out when she met charming John Warren, a storekeeper's son who worked his way up from being a stable lad to a respected bloodstock agent. They wed in 1985 and John has now become the Queen's bloodstock manager and racing adviser. As a tribute to his late father-in-law he is reluctant to call himself the Queen's Racing Manager.

Like characters from a Jilly Cooper novel, the

Queen's trainers have tended to lead colourful private lives.

Major Hern was succeeded at West Ilsley by Willie Hastings-Bass, a direct descendant of Robin Hood who became the Earl of Huntingdon. He and his wife Susan, granddaughter of legendary cricketer Sir Pelham Warner, became 'great friends' of the Queen. But in 1998 he quit his post, citing 'financial pressures' and in 2001, after 12 years of marriage, the couple divorced.

In 2006 the Queen's National Hunt trainer Nicky Henderson and his wife of 28 years, Diana, split up. Mum-of-three, Diana, then 51, moved out of the Seven Barrows stables at Lambourn, Berkshire, two years after her husband was romantically linked with Newmarket florist Sophie Waddilove. Locals jokingly renamed the stables 'Three-and-a-half Barrows' after Diana hammered out a financial settlement.

Old Etonian Nicky, 55 in 2006, would often take his elegant wife to lunch with the Queen Mother at the Cheltenham Festival, and friends were shocked at their separation.

The Queen's current principal trainer, Sir Michael Stoute, also left his wife Patricia in the early 1990s, and set up home with fellow trainer Coral Pritchard-Gordon.

In 1999 there was amazement in racing circles when it was revealed he earned more than £1 million a year, and second royal trainer Richard Hannon pocketed £763,000. Some MPs were quick to contrast the massive sums with the wages of stable lads, some of whom survive on £10,000 a year.

In December 2000 Sir Michael, a policeman's son who was born in Barbados, was searched by customs officials at London's Gatwick Airport as he went to board a flight to the Caribbean island.

They found £40,000 worth of US dollars in his suitcase, and confiscated the cash under the 1994 Drug Trafficking Act. It was later returned after he gave a satisfactory explanation, and no action was taken, but he could have done without the publicity.

Sir Michael's keen sense of humour shines through though when he frequently tells an amusing true story about himself. One day the Queen arrived early at his Freemason Lodge stables in Newmarket, Suffolk, and was given a guided tour of the grounds, before returning to the house for breakfast. Sir Michael remarked that he had some 'urgent business' to attend to and left Her Majesty in the capable hands of his partner Coral.

She suggested a tour of the house itself and took the Queen upstairs to show her around. When she got to the master bathroom, the door was locked, and she shouted: 'Who's in there – is that you, Michael?'

Not knowing that the Queen was standing

outside, Sir Michael, who was answering a call of nature, shouted back: 'Of course it ******* is, I'm having a ****.'

Her Majesty, as always, saw the funny side, and the story has now become common knowledge in racing circles.

The Queen loves going to the races, but royal engagements prevent her from seeing as much of the turf as she would like. So she was delighted a few years ago when the Racing Channel on pay TV started up, and she took out a subscription at Buckingham Palace and Windsor Castle.

In July 2006 she settled down in eager anticipation at the palace to watch her horse, Banknote, run at Haydock Park – but was met by a blank screen!

A courtier had forgotten to renew her £20-a-month fee and the service had been cut off. What made it worse was that Banknote romped home at 11-2 and she was said to be 'livid' that she couldn't see the moment of triumph.

A royal insider revealed: 'She was horrified when she pushed her remote button and nothing happened. A huge inquest was launched and the culprit was given a carpeting. Needless to say the fee was paid quickly, and the service restored just in time for her to see another of her horses, Fleeting Memory, win at Bath.'

Just as she will always have dogs, the Queen will continue to own racehorses. And after 20 years of showing little interest in the sport, Prince Charles has also got his hands on a young filly.

Encouraged by his wife the Duchess of Cornwall, Charles bought a one-year-old for around £100,000 in 2006. The horse, named Royal Superlative, by Camilla, is expected to run on the flat in 2008.

The Queen will be delighted that her son is following in her footsteps, and, of course, will tune in to watch the horse run, assuming her subscription is up-to-date!

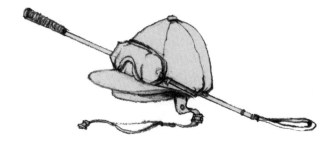

Cars: Toot! Toot! Get Out of Our Way!

*'For years Philip has travelled around the capital in a black cab,
ignoring pedestrians trying to hail him.'*

The royals have always enjoyed the open road and the delights of speeding along like Mr Toad of *The Wind in the Willows* fame. 'Faster and faster' seems to have been their motto, and almost every member of the family has been labelled an 'arrogant road hog' at some point, resulting in a plethora of crashes, shunts and brushes with the law over the years.

Although they claim to have 'gone green' in recent times, the truth is that the Windsor clan still drive expensive and powerful motors, and love putting their foot down.

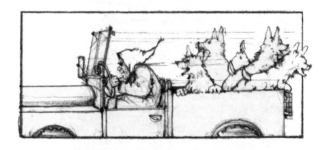

Shortly before his 1947 marriage, Prince Philip got into trouble with the police and his future father-in-law George VI when he wrecked his little MG sports car after taking a bend too quickly.

He ended up crawling from the remains in a ditch, and was apparently lucky to still be alive.

Princess Elizabeth's nanny Marion Crawford later revealed that Philip, then plain Lieutenant Mountbatten, was 'gravely cautioned by the King' about his love of speed.

Palace chauffeurs became unwilling to let Philip take out their beautifully maintained limos after they were often returned with unexplained dents and scratches. He was even stopped for racing down The Mall in London on the eve of his wedding, but cheekily escaped a fine when he explained to a bewildered policeman, 'Sorry, officer, but I've got an appointment with the Archbishop of Canterbury!'

A prang with a London black cab at Hyde Park corner perhaps gave Philip the ingenious idea of getting a taxi himself. For years he has travelled around the capital in one, ignoring pedestrians trying to hail him. Philip was years ahead of his time, realising that action was required to help the environment and cut down on fuel use. The taxis replaced a battery-driven Bedford van, and he currently has a dark green £20,000 Metrocab with room for five passengers, as well as a Range Rover for longer journeys.

Almost every member of the royal family has been stopped, questioned and even prosecuted for speeding. Even the Queen, who does not normally drive on public roads, had to apologise to a family she terrified while driving at 60 mph through a royal park in her Jaguar.

Nigel Dawson was strolling through Windsor Great Park in June 1993 with his three young sons when Her Majesty sent them diving for cover. She ignored the 30 mph speed limit and flashed by, sternly waving Nigel aside as he tried to shout at her to slow down.

Mr Dawson was so shocked that he made a complaint to the Queen's personal policeman. She accepted she was at fault and ordered her private secretary to write an apology to the family. In the letter she expressed concern at the 'alarm and inconvenience' she caused.

The Dawson family were not the only victims of the Queen's love of speed. Nurse Pat Duncan claimed she and her son Simon were nearly run down by their monarch, also in Windsor Great Park. They had to jump to safety on a grass verge as Elizabeth, with Philip sitting beside her, raced towards them at nearly 70 mph.

'She looked really sour faced and angry,' said Mrs Duncan. 'It was totally irresponsible.'

Inside her own family the Queen has a reputation for her cavalier driving. She seems oblivious to her own safety, let alone anyone else's, and tends not to wear her seat belt, which is allowed on private roads. Despite the protests of safety groups, she doesn't wear a hard hat when out riding either.

In 2001 the Queen scared the life out of Crown Prince Abdullah of Saudi Arabia when she offered to take him for a drive around the Windsor Estate. The Prince, who had never been driven by a woman before, was nervous from the start. As they drove along, the Queen kept chatting and waving her arms about, pointing out places of interest. The Prince said later that he couldn't believe his host wasn't keeping her eyes on the road all the time, as his chauffeur always did. When the trip ended he almost collapsed with relief.

And when Prince Charles heard about the adventure he laughed and remarked that he knew exactly how the poor man felt! When the Queen took delivery of an £80,000 limo in 2005, it was not the soft grain leather trim, walnut veneer and lambswool rugs that concerned her ... but the size of the parcel shelf. For that is where her corgis like to curl up while being shuttled between Windsor and Buckingham Palace.

A standard Jaguar was turned down because the shelf was not deep enough, so a Super Eight version provided the room for the dogs to travel in comfort.

Members of the royal family have been stopped many times by police for speeding, but it was not until 1969 that the authorities decided to start prosecutions.

Prince Michael of Kent was the first. He was fined that year for driving his Aston Martin at twice the limit in London's Park Lane.

In 1970 he was fined for careless driving when

his Jaguar saloon rammed a van. He was also the first royal to be banned, losing his licence for three months in 1974 after doing 110 mph in a 50 mph zone.

In 1990 he was banned again, this time for 14 days after being caught doing 103 mph. The Prince, then President of the Royal Automobile Club, made the mistake of overtaking an unmarked police car in his Aston Martin on the M4 motorway in Wiltshire.

He even got into trouble during the London to Brighton vintage car run in 1987, cutting up other motorists and speeding in an historic 1903 Gordon Bennett Napier. Five other competitors reported him to the police, and a senior officer 'had a word' about his Toad-like driving.

The Princess Royal has an unenviable reputation at the wheel.

In November 1972 Anne was given a written warning after being clocked driving at up to 90 mph on the M1, but was not prosecuted. In January 1977 she was fined £40 in Alfreton, Derbyshire for doing 96 mph, again on the M1.

And in October 1990 she was fined £150 and banned for a month by magistrates in Gloucester-shire after admitting two speeding offences, both in the same week!

In July 1990 Anne was seen racing through country lanes at 100 mph in her turbo-powered

£115,000 Bentley as she hurried between engagements. As she gathered speed Mrs Kaye Hills, wife of the High Sheriff of Gloucestershire, tried to follow behind in her Subaru.

'It was hair-raising,' she said. 'On one bend I drifted broadside. I mentioned it to the Princess later and she just laughed.'

Safety campaigners were furious. Marion Page, chairman of Keep Death Off Our Roads condemned Anne as 'irresponsible' and blasted: 'If these speeds are correct, the Princess should be arrested. It's even worse that she's a royal. Everyone else will think they can get away with the same.'

In March 2001 she was booked for her fourth offence, driving at 93 mph in a 70 mph zone. She was fined £400 and her licence was endorsed with five penalty points after telling magistrates she thought the car following her with blue flashing lights was a police escort!

The irony, of course, is that Anne and the other senior royals are always accompanied by police bodyguards, so goodness knows what conversations unfold as they flout the laws of the road.

Anne's ex-husband Captain Mark Phillips also likes to rev it up. He was banned for a week in 1996 for driving his Land Rover at 73 mph in a 40 mph area. And he was lucky to escape alive following a terrifying head-on crash in 1984.

His Range Rover was written off after colliding

with a Renault, which was overtaking a lorry on a winding country lane. Mark escaped unhurt and the other driver was only slightly injured. But the lorry driver Gerry Young said at the time: 'They were both lucky they weren't killed.'

Anne and Mark's children have both cheated death in high speed crashes.

Out of date tax discs seem to be a royal speciality.

Zara Phillips was spotted driving around in an untaxed sporty Audi S3 in January 2005. Her mum, Anne, arrived for an official engagement in an untaxed Range Rover in 1998. Both were condemned by the DVLA for being 'irresponsible'.

Princess Margaret's son, Viscount Linley, was seen riding his BMW motorbike in March 1993 with a disc that had expired a month earlier.

The Queen's nephew has also had a series of brushes with the law. In the 1980s he was banned three times for speeding and, in 1989, he was disqualified for four months and fined £150 for doing 75 mph on his motorbike in a 40 mph zone.

In January 1993 he was quizzed by police after a crash with two other bikers.

Linley has faced huge insurance bills because of his bad driving record – his offences number at least nine.

Not surprisingly he has given up driving in London, preferring to walk or take a cab. But he still managed to attract unwanted headlines in September 2006 when he was pictured riding a Strida foldaway push-bike in London, with his four-year-old daughter Margarita clinging to his back while perched on a tiny parcel rack. A couple of weeks later, after protests from safety campaigners, he had changed to a larger bike with a proper child's seat.

Another of the Queen's cousins, the Duke of Gloucester, was banned from driving for his fourth speeding offence in December 2004. He was caught doing 70 mph in a 60 mph zone and promptly offered his resignation as President of the Institute of Advanced Drivers.

The Prince of Wales has a clean licence, but he's been lucky. Despite his green credentials today, he has always enjoyed driving fast sports cars, and although he has been questioned by police, he has never been prosecuted.

His collection of cars includes an armour-plated turbo-charged Bentley, a vintage Aston Martin DB6, a £150,000 Aston Martin Volante and a diesel Range Rover. He has recently bought an environmentally friendly Toyota Prius hybrid and is converting royal cars to run on bio fuel.

His only known accident was in 1987 when he rashly overtook a coach on a private Windsor Great

Park road and hit a Range Rover, causing £1,000 damage to the side of his beloved DB6.

Charles adores the car. In 1987 he lost his temper with wife Diana for perching on the bonnet while watching him play polo. 'Get off, you'll dent it,' he told her.

The Princess was a fast but skilful driver who also managed to keep a clean licence. When she first appeared on the royal scene as a 19-year-old kindergarten teacher, she was driving a pale blue Volkswagen Polo but moved onto a Mini Metro, a gift from her fiancé Charles.

Diana got a taste for fast cars and soon into her marriage acquired a sexy red convertible Ford Escort RS 2000, capable of 120 mph.

In 1989 she swapped that for an elegant £42,000 green Jaguar XJS with a top speed of 160 mph.

As her marriage crumbled, she became the first royal to drive a foreign car in 50 years when she was offered a luxurious Mercedes 500 SL. (The royals rarely buy their own cars, and benefit from generous leasing arrangements with the manufacturers who are anxious for publicity.) Diana loved the German convertible, but felt uncomfortable not supporting British industry and returned to Jaguars.

After her separation, however, she was free to drive what she wanted, and began using a sporty Audi.

In 1994 she managed to plough into design

director Jackie Walls' BMW during a Knightsbridge shopping trip.

Diana, like Charles, had been warned by police about speeding on several occasions but was never prosecuted. Her worst speeding offence came after a disastrous trip to Korea in 1992 with Charles, shortly before they separated. When Diana's aircraft arrived back at RAF Northolt she was angry and frustrated because of her tortured private life.

She took the wheel at 6am, leaving her detective to occupy the passenger seat. The dual carriageway of the A40 into London was virtually deserted and just too tempting for her. She put her foot down and triggered a string of automatic speed cameras on the 40-minute dash back to her London apartment in Kensington Palace.

The back-up police car behind struggled to keep up as Diana powered her way home. If she had been prosecuted she would have accumulated enough points to lose her licence, but the incident was swept under the carpet and no action was taken.

Diana also broke the law frequently by flagrantly parking on yellow lines all over London.

In 1996 she walked away from a terrifying five car smash outside London's Natural History Museum. The Princess was driving a borrowed BMW, which was wrecked, as was a high performance Porsche. The accident was not her fault and she left the scene hurriedly in a taxi after speaking to police.

In 1997 the world was shocked when Diana died in a Paris car crash with her then boyfriend Dodi Fayed. Official investigations by the French and British concluded the accident was caused by the drunk-driving at high speed of chauffeur Henri Paul, who also perished. Reports also said Diana might have lived had she been wearing her seat-belt.

Cars once owned by Diana now fetch top prices when they come up for sale.

The Duchess of York had a lucky escape after a dramatic hit-and-run motorway smash in 1988. Fergie, who was then just three weeks from giving birth to her first daughter Beatrice, was a front seat passenger in her own red Jaguar XJS when it was hit in the side by a Ford Fiesta travelling in the opposite direction in road works on the M4 near Newbury in Berkshire. The car was badly damaged but Sarah was unhurt. The other driver was later prosecuted for careless driving and failing to stop after an accident.

The younger royals seem determined to do their bit for the history of motoring madness in the monarchy.

Zara Phillips may be a world champion on horseback but in December 2000 she was breathalysed by police after crashing her £17,000 Land Rover. The Queen's granddaughter, then 19, was left shaken and suffered cuts and bruises to her face after her car left the road and hit a wall in Gloucestershire. The breath test proved negative and she wasn't prosecuted, but the car was a write-off.

Zara's brother Peter Phillips walked away from a horror crash in which his car was sent rolling across the road. He was on his way to China's first ever Grand Prix Formula One race in Shanghai in September 2004 when his vehicle was hit by a speeding car. He emerged shaken but with only a minor bump to his head. Passengers with him suffered broken bones and cuts and were taken to hospital.

Princes William and Harry both love speed and danger, and both have been publicly slated for arrogant driving.

Harry was branded a reckless 'boy racer' by worried army mums in July 2006, who feared for their children's safety as the Prince regularly disregarded the speed limit on his base at Bovington in Dorset.

Mother-of-two Sandra McGhee said: 'Harry drives his black sporty Audi A3 around the barracks like a maniac. The boy needs to slow down before there is a serious accident.'

But royal watchers were hardly surprised by his antics. After all, Harry would drive cars around royal estates as he was growing up and he and

William were frequent lovers of go-kart racing from a young age. Harry was even once spotted shooting birds with an air rifle through the sun roof of a moving car.

Wealthy landowner Earl Bathurst claimed William behaved like a yob in a road rage incident in June 2003. Prince Charles ordered his son to apologise after learning that Will, driving a black VW Golf, overtook the Earl's Land Rover at speed on a private road leaving Cirencester Polo Club. The Earl, who has a £35 million fortune, said: 'I don't care who it is, royalty or not, speeding is not allowed on my estate.'

William's motoring has yet to land him in trouble with the law and he seems determined to keep things that way with a legal speed camera detector fixed to his dashboard. The £400 Road Angel helps drivers to avoid all three types of speed cameras in Britain, as well as hand-held radars and camera vans. Prince Harry also has the laser device on his car.

But William's love of motorbikes is already causing him problems with the police – ironically his own protection officers! In 2004 he bought himself a £7,000, 157 mph Daytona 600, described as a 'rocket on two wheels'.

Despite the misgivings of Prince Charles and the Queen, William has become addicted to the thrill of 'going solo'. In particular he loves the fact that in his helmet and black leathers, no-one recognises him, and while on the bike he feels totally free.

After two years he moved onto a 175 mph, 1100cc Honda Blackbird. But after a 'wobble' in late 2006 when he nearly came off, officers warned their superiors that they would not break the law when shadowing him.

At any one time William is guarded by two armed policemen – one riding pillion – on a motorcycle. But increasingly they have found it difficult to keep up with him without putting themselves in danger.

One insider said: 'It is not on motorways that he is at risk, but in urban areas where speed restrictions are more in force. As well as keeping up with him and being alert to possible dangers, officers are concerned in case they break the speed limits. If the Prince speeds they either do the same or let him go off on his own.'

William has shrugged off the problem, insisting that he cannot be wrapped in cotton wool. 'Riding a motorbike can be dangerous, but so can lots of things really,' he said in an interview. 'Admittedly, there are more risks involved in riding a motorbike than there are with other things. It is a risk, but as long as you've had sufficient and thorough training you should be okay. You've just got to be aware of what you're doing.'

A Family Christmas: Just What One Always Wanted

'The royals have their own bespoke crackers.'

As she tore open the wrapping paper of a present left under the 20-foot high Christmas tree at Sandringham, the Queen's face lit up. She proudly held up a plain white cooking apron and cooed with delight. The most famous woman in the world, who could buy anything she wants, just loves worthless 'joke' gifts.

Then she opened another, this time a plastic shower hat emblazoned with the phrase 'Ain't life a bitch!'

She looked round the room for the culprit and pointed an accusing finger at her grandson Prince Harry, as everyone else in the room collapsed with laughter. Later Charles and Diana's younger son told army pals that Her Majesty loved the gift, and often wore it for her morning ablutions.

Such silly presents are a tradition among the adults in the House of Windsor, who regularly exchange trinkets worth as little as a few pounds. On these festive occasions the Queen has unwrapped little doormats, whoopee cushions and even pots and pans.

One former servant revealed: 'When you already have everything, expensive gifts don't mean much. The royals prefer to get something which makes them laugh, or a small practical gadget rather than something worth thousands of pounds.'

Prince Philip loves novelty items like unusual can-openers and corkscrews for family barbecues at Balmoral, where he often does the cooking.

The Queen has given 'singing fishes' to some of her friends and family after she was presented with a Big Mouth Billy Bass, which is set on a grand piano at Balmoral. She finds the US-designed toy, which has sold millions worldwide, hilarious.

At the start of their marriage, Charles and Diana entered into the spirit of things and exchanged amusing presents. She gave him some Mickey Mouse socks, and he rewarded his fashion conscious wife with a tatty hat which an aide had bought for a pound in a charity shop.

One of Charles's favourite gifts was a white leather loo seat.

Royal children have always been given proper treats, and no expense is spared. Jewellery, bicycles, hunting rifles, mobile phones, fishing rods, computers and even puppies and ponies have been favourites among the youngsters.

No event in the royal calendar is more traditional than the Christmas celebrations at Sandringham. The sprawling 20,000-acre estate in Norfolk is the Queen's private property and it becomes her base for the festive season until February each year.

There have been rumours that some members of the family like Charles and his sons would like to move the annual gathering back to Windsor Castle, where royal Christmases used to be held many years ago, but they have so far proved incorrect.

Before the Queen departs for Norfolk, a lavish ball is held at Buckingham Palace for the royals and servants to let their hair down together. Elizabeth and Philip give their staff presents, which they choose themselves from a catalogue, and the price range depends on seniority. Servants queue up to receive their gifts, and a thank you from the Queen for another year's hard work.

The Queen also carries on the delightful tradition of her father and grandfather and distributes Christmas puddings – almost 1500 – to a wide range of staff at all the royal households. (In recent years these have been ordered in bulk from Tesco to save money.)

The Queen and her husband of 60 years send off Christmas cards, which normally feature a family photo, signed 'Elizabeth R' and 'Philip' with the date of the year. (Her Majesty sends out 750 cards, and of course receives thousands, but only those from family and close friends are displayed.) She begins the mammoth task of signing them at the beginning of December, sitting down at a Palace table with a gold and onyx fountain pen, which belonged to her father George VI.

At her side she has special blotting paper on

which imprints of words cannot be read for security reasons, and any half-written letters are shredded.

Personal cards are signed 'With love from Mummy and Papa' to their four children, 'Granny and Gramps' to their grandchildren and 'Lilibet and Philip' to other family members.

Everyone else gets 'Elizabeth R' and some are now signed with an 'autopen', which produces a realistic facsimile.

The Queen likes Christmas to be the same every year because it brings back happy childhood memories.

She arrives at Sandringham a couple of days before Christmas Eve and personally supervises the preparation of rooms for her family guests. In the White Drawing-Room servants decorate the Norfolk spruce, felled from the estate, with Queen Victoria's antique angels and shiny baubles. But the Queen always finishes it off with tinsel and a large star, just as her father once did.

On Christmas Eve the entire family gathers, and dog fights permitting, takes tea at 4pm in the wood-panelled drawing-room. Sandwiches, home-baked scones, muffins and cakes are washed down with Earl Grey tea and a special Indian blend.

Everyone then retires to their rooms for a rest before returning at 6pm in the White Drawing-Room.

All the presents are carefully placed on cloth-covered trestle tables, with a name card marking each family member's pile of gifts. Then, just as the monarch has done since Queen Victoria first started the German tradition of opening presents on Christmas Eve, the Queen gives the signal and everyone dives in.

Princess Margaret's son Viscount Linley has described this scene as 'total uproar' with great shrieks of laughter greeting the unveilings.

After the gifts have been opened, the royals retire for a bath and the first of many clothes changes. (When the Duchess of York was still in favour, she described Christmas as 'exhausting' – not least because over 24 hours she wore seven different outfits!)

At 8pm everyone gathers for pre-prandial drinks and the Queen arrives for a dry Martini at about 8.15pm.

Fergie recalled: 'You never let the Queen beat you down for dinner, end of story – to come in any later would be unimaginably disrespectful.'

The Christmas Eve banquet is a grand occasion with the men dressed in black tie and the ladies in gowns.

A typical dinner will be Norfolk shrimps, lamb or game shot on the estate and a pudding of soufflé or tarte tartin.

White wine is served with the starter, claret with

the main course, and champagne with the pudding. The family all toast each other as they clink their champagne glasses. But ironically few of them actually like the stuff, and most gets finished off by the servants as they clear the table afterwards!

The royals have their own bespoke crackers, with gold or silver crowns, containing the normal useless novelties and corny jokes. The Queen is the only person who doesn't don her party paper hat, but she does love reading out the one-liners.

At around 10pm the ladies take coffee in another room while Prince Philip offers port and brandy to the gentlemen. They later meet up again for more drinks but the Queen tends to be in bed by midnight, leaving younger members to carry on the fun.

On Christmas morning the family walk to the nearby church of St Mary Magdalene for a service at 11am. It is one of the few occasions when all the royal family are seen together informally. Hundreds of estate workers and their families, together with locals, used to queue to see them, especially in the days of Diana, but numbers are now well down.

Inside, holly from the Queen's woodland decorates the silver altar and there is a tree in the nave.

For the collection, the Queen, Philip and Charles each give a £10 note that has been ironed and folded by a valet so that the monarch's head faces outwards.

The brisk walk in the cold air back to the house is rewarded with a cocktail or some mulled wine in the grand cream and gold drawing-room before lunch.

Scarlet liveried footmen serve a traditional lunch using the Copeland white and blue dinner service bearing George V and Queen Mary's monogram.

Queen Victoria's gargantuan Christmas feasts at Windsor Castle used to include a 60 lb baron of beef, which four men turned on a spit for ten hours, 50 turkeys, 40 geese and a stuffed boar's head. But the present royals eat like the rest of Britain and enjoy turkey with chestnuts, herb stuffing and cranberry sauce with all the trimmings.

The servants leave the room while they are eating and then enter with the Christmas pudding flaming in brandy. There is no hanging about, and the entire meal is scoffed down in 90 minutes so that everyone can watch Her Majesty's Christmas message to the nation on TV at 3pm. The whole family watches in absolute silence, and at the end Prince Philip toasts his wife and raises a glass of brandy to 'Her Majesty, the Queen'. (In 2006 it was reported that in recent years the Queen has actually become self-conscious about her performance and watches it on her own in a separate room, but courtiers refused to confirm this rumour.)

The evening meal is a much lighter event and, on the Queen's orders, Christmas pudding is nowhere to be seen. Former royal chef Graham Newbould said: 'The family are not keen on it or mince pies, so I could be quite bold with other desserts.'

A highly intoxicating chilled pina colada mousse with a raspberry coulis made with a large slug of rum always goes down well, while a cold lobster salad topped with caviar is a favourite starter.

The royals help themselves to cold turkey and other leftovers from a buffet table for the main course.

Afterwards the TV remains firmly off and everyone plays games. The Queen loves charades and is an excellent mimic, particularly of political figures she knows only too well. She is apparently brilliant at former Russian leader Boris Yeltsin, Tony Blair and various US Presidents.

They also play board games like Trivial Pursuit and Monopoly, and one year Who Wants to be a Millionaire went down a storm, according to servants overhearing the banter.

Blind Man's Buff is an old-fashioned favourite. Ex-employee Charles Oliver recalled that one Christmas, a blindfolded Queen Mum heard a rustle behind the curtains and groped her way towards the sound. She embraced the lurking figure with a hug and kiss as the rest of the family shrieked with laughter. When she took the blindfold off she saw she had cuddled a footman who had come in with some drinks!

Breakfast on Boxing Day is a filling buffet of kedgeree, bacon and eggs, cereals and toast to set the men up for the traditional shoot.

Prince Philip organises the trudge across cold, muddy fields and is joined by keen marksmen Charles, William, Harry, Edward and Peter Phillips. Golf-mad Andrew is not so keen on shooting, riding or skiing.

The Queen and the other wives follow along. picking up pheasants, partridges and the occasional

duck. Almost every year she seems to be photo-
graphed wringing the neck of an injured bird, much
to the annoyance of animal welfare groups.

Lunch is taken in a plain wooden hut surrounded
by trees in the heart of the estate. The family clusters
around a smelly paraffin heater, and they tuck into
a buffet of cold meats, hot sausages, soup and salads,
with spirits and tea to warm them up.

If the weather is good the Queen will sometimes
go for a walk with her dogs on the beach near
Hunstanton, while the men continue their shoot.

It's the same every year – and always will be
while she is monarch.